THE MIND CHANGERS

THE MIND

Emory A. Griffin

CHANGERS

The Art of Christian Persuasion

Tyndale House
Publishers, Inc.
Wheaton, Illinois

Seventh printing, July 1983

THE MIND CHANGERS
Cover cartoon © *PUNCH* (Rothco).
Library of Congress Catalog Card Number 76-44649
ISBN 0-8423-4290-7, paper.
Copyright © 1976 by Tyndale House Publishers, Inc.,
Wheaton, Illinois.
Printed in the United States of America.

To my wonderful wife, Jeanie,
whose love, warmth, and affirmation
free me to take the risk
of trying to influence others,

and

to my great kids, Jim and Sharon,
who have taught me much about the
subtle art of influence and
aren't afraid to have me write it down.

CONTENTS

ACKNOWLEDGMENTS

MY PARENTS

RUTH FLESVIG GIBSON

AL JENKINS

KEN PIKE

ED CARNELL

BILL STARR

AL GOLDBERG

BILL ENRIGHT

LYNN OEFFLING

MY STUDENTS

If these people hadn't been, this book wouldn't have been.

who first gave me the desire to try to change the world.

her excitement for the Lord drew me into the faith.

a pastor who spent a lot of time sharing himself with a young Christian.

of Wycliffe Bible Translators; my Gamaliel, at whose feet I'd gladly sit again.

a great and sensitive man of God at Fuller Seminary; he was willing to show me his humanness.

my mentor in Young Life; he taught me the fantastic power of praise and encouragement.

a delightful prof in grad school who let me catch the fun of doing research in persuasion.

my close friend and pastor who puts so much of this book into practice.

a colleague at Wheaton who read, questioned, encouraged, typed, and prodded until the book was complete.

who convinced me that I had something worthwhile to say.

OVERVIEW

Almost Persuaded*

I'm writing this the day after Christmas. My six-year-old daughter, Sharon, had asked Santa Claus for a candle-making kit, and yesterday it showed up on schedule. At 6:30 in the morning she burst into our room and announced that she and I were going to make a candle.

The kit contained large, flat sheets of colored wax and string to be used as a wick. The directions indicated that candle-making is a three-step process. First, you place the wax in an oven to heat it until it's soft and pliable. Then you take it out of the oven, roll it around a wick, and mold it into any shape that pleases. Finally, you place the completed candle in cold water until it becomes hard. Unfortunately neither Sharon nor I bothered with the written instructions on our first attempts.

As soon as my daughter drew one of the thin, brittle sheets of wax from the carton, she tried to force it into the shape of a turtle—the shape that was shown on the box. The results were predictable—many shattered pieces of wax and many tears of frustration.

I confidently showed Sharon that the wax had to be melted first. After it had been in the oven ten minutes, I was able to shape it. Follow-

*A portion of this chapter was originally published as an article in the Crawford Broadcasting Company Program Guide, Spring—Summer, 1973.

ing a number of futile attempts to form various animals, I settled on a rather stylish looking letter S, in honor of my daughter's first initial. The wax, however, was still very soft. Every time I took my hands away from the material, it sank under its own weight into a nondescript mass. It was at this point that we sought the guidance of the printed instructions and ultimately produced an object of art.

I have taken you through this tale of candle-making because it occurs to me that it is helpful in understanding the way in which people are persuaded. Like making that candle, significant persuasion involves a three-step process:

$$MELT \rightarrow MOLD \rightarrow MAKE\ HARD$$

You may notice that the first two words have just one syllable and begin with M. I haven't been able to think of a short M word which means "to solidify." After reading the rest of the chapter, try to think of a word which adequately describes the process.

Before discussing the three steps, let me explain what I mean by significant persuasion. One requirement is that the change be longlasting—that it persist over time. We're all familiar with the type of religious experience that starts out like gangbusters, but soon fizzles out. This kind of witness brings dishonor to God and bitterness to the fellow who changed his mind. A few years ago I was shook by the frank admission of a high school fellow at a summer camp. "I know all about this Christian stuff, Em," he confided. "I asked Christ into my life when I was eleven years old. I was a Christian for a few years, but it was too hard and I didn't get nothin' out of it. So I told God to get back out of my life." Jesus' parable of the sower makes it clear that a faith which doesn't last over time is worthless.

Change in behavior is another condition for meaningful influence. Jesus places a premium on our deeds when he says: "Why do you call me 'Lord, Lord,' and not do what I tell you?" And again, "If you love me, you will keep my commandments." A man's actions speak so loud we can't hear what he's saying. Now it's true that behavior can lag behind intentions. But it's silly to claim we've had a major influence on a person's life if he doesn't eventually alter the way he acts. Persuasion that fails to break out into behavior is trivial.

There's a final test for successful persuasion. It's based on the fact that our crucial attitudes aren't held in a vacuum—they're interrelated. Any substantial change in my relationship with God is going to force me to reevaluate both my opinion of others and my own self-image. A vital change in one area of life will seep into related areas. True conversion affects not only our "religious" responses, but other attitudes as well.

Our Christian lingo reflects the importance of these criteria. The short-term convert is labeled a "backslider." The man whose behavior doesn't match his words is scathingly called a "hypocrite." When a person refuses to let his faith in God broaden out into other activities, we dismiss him as a "Sunday Christian." If, on the other hand, our attempts at influence bring about a widespread, permanent, behavioral change, then we've really got persuasion worth talking about.

MELT. Most people don't want to be persuaded—of anything! "Don't confuse me with the facts, my mind's made up." They seem to have a built-in antagonism toward anyone trying to change their attitudes or behavior. I know that I usually feel obstinate when talking with car salesmen, skeptical when viewing ads on TV, and resistant when hearing a speaker present an opposing viewpoint. In the field of persuasion, this is called "psychological reactance." If someone tries to push us, we push back.

The Bible speaks of people being hardened toward the Lord. Wax cannot be molded when it's hard. It has to be melted first. So do people. Our attempts to influence another person often fail because he remains frozen or locked into a fixed position.

Let's suppose that we try to present the gospel to an ordinary man who is frozen in a non-Christian position. A person tends to expose himself only to those messages with which he already agrees. Because of this selective exposure, he probably won't hear our message in the first place. He will be deaf to our radio program, blind to our tract, and absent from our meeting.

Even if we crash into his life and get him to listen to our words, he'll continue to resist. As he hears our message, he will be actively counterarguing each point. Perhaps we will persist in our effort, feeling that this might be the only time he will hear about the Lord. Unfortunately, our high-pressure tactics may guarantee that fact. The more a person thinks up reasons for not believing, the more he becomes immune to even a winsome presentation of the gospel.

What can we do to make people open to influence? How can we melt them so that they will at least consider the Christian message? We can be human!

As long as we seek to impress others that we are right and they are wrong, we will merely drive them away. If we treat others as souls to be won for our side instead of as human beings who are worthwhile in their own right, we create resistance to the gospel. If, on the other hand, we honestly admit our own faults and doubts, others will lower the barriers which they have raised. Paradoxically, we have the most influence on people when we are the least manipulative. Perhaps this is part of Jesus' meaning when he told the evangelists to be wise as serpents and harmless as doves.

MOLD. Once Sharon and I learned how to soften the wax, we had fun shaping a candle. The most important part of this operation was feedback. Every few seconds we compared what we had made with our image of what we wanted to make. Needless to say, the two were never the same, but the continual testing helped us mold a candle which we thought was rather nice.

As Christian persuaders, we often fail to check the results of our message. We blithely quote, "God's Word will not return void," and automatically assume that what we said was effective. Perhaps our reluctance to measure the response is due to our secret fear of failure. I face this in my teaching. When I think I have really "bombed" a class lecture, I tend to avoid questions or comments from my students. Such feedback is embarrassing, but of course it also gives me a clue as to how I should do it the next time.

I recently heard a clergyman say, "The times are so important that we can't afford to fail." These words bothered me, because if it's true that we can't afford to fail, we'll be scared to take an honest look at what we're accomplishing. We'll never learn from our mistakes. I'd rather think of it this way: "The times are so important that we *must* be willing to fail." We must risk failure in order to discover new ways of getting people to consider Jesus Christ.

"Goodness, what do you suppose the Rector's message for the troubled world was this time?"

My daughter and I discovered that molding a candle is not a five-minute job. You can't rush—it takes lots of time and patience. Just as shaping a candle is a gradual process, so it is with the process of social influence. I realize that this runs counter to the typical image of Christian persuasion. We expect sudden conversions and blinding flashes of insight. But actual experience suggests that such instances are the exceptions rather than the rule.

Think back through your past and pick the one person who's had the greatest impact on your Christian life. Chances are you'll select someone who's had an ongoing influence rather than a one-shot blitz effect. For me, that man was Ken Pike, a Christian linguistics professor at the University of Michigan. I wasn't enrolled in his course, but we played water polo together three times a week during my senior year. We'd talk as we walked together to the pool, then play an exhausting thirty-minute game with ten other men, and finally all go out for a relaxed lunch as a group. Twenty years later I can look back and see my world view changing over the course of those months as he gently nudged me to consider new ideas. Molding a life takes time.

MAKE HARD. A new belief is like hot wax—it can't support itself until it becomes firm. Sharon solidified our "objet d'art" by immersing it in a bowl of water. The natural buoyancy of the water held the soft wax in the shape that we'd formed. A newfound faith is equally vulnerable and needs to be propped up. In most cases this *external* support must come from a community of like-minded believers. It's too much to expect a young Christian to stand firm in total isolation.

My own experience bears this out. For the past fifteen years, I've led a Young Life club. During this time I've seen hundreds of high school kids who had no Christian background accept Christ. Almost without exception, those who have found a Christian friend, joined a church, or married a Christian have continued on in the faith. Those who have tried to go it on their own have vanished. It's not without reason that Christ sent the seventy out two by two.

Our candle gained *internal* strength as it was suspended in the cool water. After a while, it didn't even need an outside pressure to hold its shape—it could stand firm by itself. A person who has been melted and molded to a new position is in a similar situation. External social support can help sustain his new faith long enough for him to begin generating his own inner reasons for believing. But he needs to develop his own new patterns of thought rather quickly. Otherwise he'll revert back to old ways of thinking when the bolstering effect of sympathetic friends is lost.

There's a frightening image in Scripture of a dog returning to his own vomit (2 Peter 2:22). The implications for the Christian persuader are clear. Persuasion is incomplete until the new belief is solidified both from within and without and becomes resistant to the molding forces of the world.

WHO'S AT WORK: GOD OR MAN? In the book of Acts we read that the Apostle Paul made his Christian defense before King Agrippa. The king's response to Paul's witness was hopeful. "Almost thou persuadest me to become a Christian," Agrippa announced. But the fact is that the king *wasn't* persuaded—he didn't join the ranks of believers. Why not? Was it just a matter of Agrippa's hardness of heart? Did Paul come up short in the way he tried to influence the king? Or did human failings have nothing to do with it? Perhaps the Holy Spirit simply declined to draw Agrippa to Jesus Christ. This is a tough area. It's hard to say precisely what the relationship is between our persuasive appeal and the urgings of the Holy Spirit in getting someone to respond to God. The closest parallel I can think of is physical healing.

When I hurt, I go to a doctor. This doesn't mean that I doubt that all healing comes ultimately from God. I firmly believe that God can mend a bone or cure a cancer without recourse to human aid. But I also believe that God normally chooses to let men play a part in the process. Doctors study long years in order to discover the principles of health that God has built into his universe. This increased knowledge of bodily functions helps the doctor to be effective.

I'm thankful that our family physician is a Christian. His genuine love for my family is revealed in the time he's willing to spend taking care of my family's physical and psychological needs. It was comforting to pray together for God's help before he wheeled me into the operating room for abdominal surgery. But I must admit that I'd already checked the diplomas on the office wall to make sure that he knew which end of the scalpel to hold. I not only want my physician to be warm and loving—I want him to be knowledgeable and competent.

I think it's the same in the field of Christian influence. God is sovereign. He doesn't *need* us. He could influence men directly if it so pleased him. But for whatever reason, he has chosen us as his ambassadors, usually making his appeal to men through us. We can be humanly competent as we seek to persuade, or we can butcher the job. God can overrule our bumbling efforts, but it's irresponsible to expect him to do so if we haven't taken the trouble to discover the best possible means of persuasion. In persuasion, as in medicine, there's a pattern of cause and effect relationships which God seems to use to achieve his ends. As Christian persuaders, it behooves us to learn these principles so that we'll be cooperating with the Holy Spirit rather than working against him. It's to that end that this book is dedicated.

WHAT'S COMING NEXT? The purpose of this book is to examine specific techniques which facilitate persuasion. In each chapter I've tried to use lots of examples to illustrate how the current findings of persuasion research can be applied to Christian witness and nurture. Because we care about a man's inner response, Chapter 2 will deal with the nature of attitudes. This is followed by a discussion in Chapter 3 of the ethical responsibilities involved in trying to change someone's way of life. Most books on persuasion consider ethics in a few tacked-on pages, but the moral issues are too important to be treated in such an offhand manner. After these introductory chapters, you'll find a section on each of the steps of persuasion.

The section on melting starts with a chapter on overcoming another's resistance to persuasion, and then considers the techniques of using guilt, fear, and role play. The section on molding looks first at positive and negative incentives as a method of shaping response, and then presents chapters on credibility, how to present a message, and the use of mass media. The section on solidifying the effects of persuasion deals with ways to prevent a new change of belief, how to alter behavior, and conformity to social pressure.

The final chapter of the book is a personal look at the effects of persuasion on the persuader and those around him. We often think of the influence process as a one-way street. I do something to someone else in order to change his life. But that's not how it works. When I made a candle with Sharon, I ended up with wax under my fingernails. The change agent is affected by his own message and by the one he seeks to change.

*　*　*　*

It's evening now. Tonight our family ate by candlelight. The soft light we enjoyed at our meal made the process of melting—molding—making solid well worth the effort. Jesus says that we are the light of the world. We can now understand that men need to be melted before they can be helped—and that after they're affected by the gospel, we must help them solidify their newfound faith. This realization will aid us in effectively getting men to consider Jesus Christ and encouraging them to grow in his love.

2

The Target

Perhaps you're familiar with the type of toy gun that shoots plastic darts. The darts are tipped with rubber suction cups so that they'll stick to a flat surface. My son, Jim, once had a gun like this. One night he asked me to come down to the basement to applaud his marksmanship. He had drawn four rather small bull's-eye targets on our large blackboard, and in the very center of each target was a dart. I was suitably impressed with his ability until he laughingly told me that he'd first shot the darts at the board, and then drawn the targets around the spots they hit.

This story illustrates many attempts at Christian influence. The gospel is sent out with little knowledge of who the target audience is, and with only a murky idea of the desired response. We often bash ahead—delivering our message with a casual unawareness of how it is being received. We comfort ourselves by quoting, "God's Word will not return void." Just as my son was satisfied with any shot he made, we are tempted to consider any response to our persuasion as evidence of success. Let's face it—we're afraid that a searching analysis of the results will show how much we've missed the mark in our attempt to influence.

We need to have some criterion or standard by which to judge the effectiveness of our outreach. Otherwise we have no way of telling whether our persuasion is helping or hurting the cause of Christ. The problem is that God doesn't put spots on foreheads, halos over hair, or even necessarily a gleam in the eye of those who respond to our proclamation of the gospel. In fact, it's probably a good thing that he doesn't. A readily discernible sign could make those who have it intolerant of those who don't, as well as making them complacent in their efforts to be more Christlike. The lack of such a sign, however, forces us to rely on the traditional measures of persuasion. These measures are: 1) changes in a person's outward behavior, and 2) changes in his inner attitude.

Behavior change provides satisfying evidence of successful persuasion. It is readily observable and often dramatic. We can see the effectiveness of Jesus' ministry by viewing the behavior of his listeners. Peter leaves his nets, Zacchaeus comes down from his tree, the blind man washes in the pool of Siloam. It's obvious that Jesus placed a premium on action. In the parable of the two sons (Matthew 21), a father asked his two sons to work in the vineyard. One said he would, but he didn't. The other said he wouldn't, but he did. Our Lord makes it clear that despite his reluctance, the second son is approved because of his actions. It's not without reason that the history of the early church is called the *Acts* of the Apostles.

Behavior change is such an important indicator of influence that many people refer to the field of persuasion as a behavioral science. I share this view. One of the later chapters will focus entirely on methods to encourage change in behavior. As I stated in Chapter 1, persuasion which never affects a person's actions seems trivial. But it also seems to me that outward appearance is not the whole story. Public compliance and private acceptance can be two different things.

The term "attitude" refers to what is going on within the inner man. "What do you honestly believe? Are you really convinced? Is your heart really in this? Are you just going through the motions?" We ask these questions because we're aware that there is an interiority to man that is not readily seen through his behavior. This interior space—this area of attitude—is vitally important to the Christian persuader. "...for the Lord sees not as man sees; man looks on the outward appearance, but the Lord looks on the heart" (1 Samuel 16:7).

"I'm only a hardhat outside. Inside, I'm squushy, tender, and a bleeding-heart liberal."

Since a person's attitude toward God is one of the twin targets of our persuasion, we'll take a look at attitude structure and strength in the rest of the chapter. In the process we'll discover what you may have suspected already—that attitudes are hard to change.

The substance H_2O has three different facets. We're most familiar with it as a liquid—water. But to fully understand H_2O we must also study its properties when it is a solid—ice, and in its gaseous state—steam. Persuasion research has shown that attitudes also have three facets. These are—what a person *thinks*, what he *feels*, and what he *plans to do*. More technically, they are referred to as cognitive belief, emotional affect, and behavioral intention. We can be confident that we've changed someone's opinion only when there's a shift in each of these three areas. Viewing these components graphically, we might say that social influence comes to a man through his head, his heart, and his hands.

BELIEFS. When I say the word "dog," what comes to mind? Do you picture a Saint Bernard or a toy poodle? Does the word conjure up an image of an animal pointing to pheasant in the field, pulling a sled through the Yukon snow, guiding a blind man across the street? Or is the dog you picture lying by a fire, chasing a cat, or guarding your home against intruders? Our mental associations reveal our beliefs, and beliefs are an important part of attitudes.

You can observe a good deal of my attitude toward dogs from a catalogue of my beliefs. When I think of the class of animal called "dog," I call up an image of our family's bassett hound. Here are my beliefs:

Dogs like to chew.
Dogs are always hungry.
Dogs sleep a lot.
Dogs can be trained to go outside.
Dogs like tummy rubs.
Dogs understand your tone of voice, but not the words.
Dogs are not very intelligent.

Notice that this list is fairly neutral in tone. It doesn't reveal whether I'm glad or sad that dogs like to chew. It merely says that I believe it is so. If someone convinced me that dogs don't like to chew, I might treat Bowser differently. Whereas he is now confined to the kitchen, he would have the run of the house.

Beliefs affect attitudes. This is true with a person's beliefs about God. There's a story about a kindergarten teacher who asked a boy what he was drawing. Without pausing to look up, he said, "A picture of God." The teacher smiled and responded, "But nobody knows what God looks like." The boy carefully put down his crayon, looked her squarely in the eye, and declared, "After I'm finished here they will." Most of us don't have an image of God quite that certain, but whatever picture we have reveals our beliefs. Is God omnipotent or powerless, omniscient or unseeing, loving or mean, just or capricious? Our theological beliefs shape our attitude toward God.

Scripture emphasizes the importance of having right beliefs about Jesus Christ. John flatly states that he is trying to affect the beliefs of his readers. "These are written that you may believe that Jesus is the Christ, the Son of God" (John 20:31). Jesus is indignant when confronted by non-belief. The epileptic boy's father pleads, "If you can do anything, have pity on us and help us." Jesus retorts, "If you can! All things are possible to him who believes" (Mark 9:22, 23) The epistles of Paul, John, and Peter caution Christians against wrong beliefs.

These lessons have not been lost on the church. Throughout the centuries, orthodox believers have stressed the importance of creeds, catechisms, covenants, doctrinal statements, and confessions of faith. It's not without reason that we sometimes refer to Christians as "believers." Rightness of belief has often been made a test of fellowship. But beliefs are only part of attitudes. It's quite possible that two people could have the same belief about God, but have different attitudes. As James scathingly states: "You believe that God is one; you do well. Even the demons believe—and shudder" (James 2:19).

The other night I spoke to a group of high school kids about God. The main point of my message was that God knows our name—that he is aware of and interested in each individual. After the talk, two guys came up to speak with me. Although they both believed me when I said that God knew their name, they had opposite reactions to this fact. One said, "Isn't it great that God cares for me personally?" The other responded, "I don't like that! It bothers me that God knows what I'm doing." This illustrates that there's more to attitudes than just belief. Feelings are equally important.

FEELINGS. It's been said that there are two kinds of people in this world—dog lovers and cat lovers. I'm sure there's a third category of those who couldn't care less. As for me, I'm a dog lover. Mention the word *dog* and I get a warm feeling inside. I want to feel a wet nose pressing against my face and toss my arms around a furry body. Cats, on the other hand, leave me cold. These emotional reactions have very little to do with my cognitive beliefs about either dogs or cats. They are simply feelings that have built up through experiences with animals. They may not be rational, but they're an important part of my attitude. In like manner, a person's "gut reaction" to God goes a long way in shaping his attitude.

People respond to God with a variety of emotions. Awe, fear, joy, guilt, warmth, boredom, humor, disgust, anger, and surprise are a few of the feelings I've heard expressed recently. Jesus seemed to think that emotions were an important part of our attitude toward him. "For whoever is ashamed of me and of my words, of him will the Son of man be ashamed when he comes in his glory'' (Luke 9:26). His disciples were indignant when a woman anointed him with expensive ointment poured from an alabaster flask. But Jesus praised her emotional outpouring as a beautiful act of devotion (Matthew 26:6-13). He also condemned the church at Laodicea for its lukewarm feelings and urged its members to be passionate in their service for him (Revelation 3:14-22).

The Christian church has had a difficult time appealing equally to beliefs and feelings. Some fellowships de-emphasize emotions to the point where any display of affect is suspect. These groups place a high value on the written and spoken arts because language communicates propositional truth. But they tend to feel uncomfortable with drama, painting, and music, since these areas evoke a deep emotional response. Other fellowships regard emotional experience as the only true sign of conversion. They place a premium on the outward expressions of devotion shown in tears of grief or shouts of joy. Having warm vibrations toward Jesus is seen as much more crucial than having a right view of the Trinity.

The point I want to make here is that the cognitive and the affective are equally important parts of attitude. There's a story about two men in a lifeboat who argue about how to get to shore. One says that the only important thing is to determine the direction they should go. The other man says that it doesn't make any difference where they head, the important thing is to row. We smile, because it's obvious that both emphases are needed to bring the boat safely to shore.

In like manner, a person needs both direction (belief) and movement (emotion) to get to God. Belief alone is dry and sterile. Emotion alone can be mere gushiness or sentimentality. Jesus illustrated this last statement when a woman in the crowd raised her voice and said, ''Blessed is the womb that bore you, and the breasts that you sucked.'' He puts emotion in proper perspective as he responds, ''Blessed rather are those who hear the word of God and keep it'' (Luke 11:28). The statement also introduces the third facet of attitude— behavioral intention.

INTENDED ACTION. The standard definition of an attitude is ''a predisposition to act.'' This suggests that attitudes are urges within us that are primed to break out into future action. You can tell a great deal of my attitude toward dogs by how I plan to treat them in the future. For instance, I'm going to feed our dog twice a day. When I come home tonight, I intend to wrestle with him on the floor. If he were to run away, I'd go search the neighborhood to try and bring him back. When he dies, I picture myself getting another dog. I may not actually end up doing all of these things, but the fact that I intend to, reveals much of my attitude toward dogs.

The same is also true of my response toward God. Do I plan to go to church, contribute to missions, give a cup of cold water to someone in need, have a daily time of prayer, give an account of the hope that is within me? Behavioral intentions, just as much as beliefs and feelings, are part of my total attitude toward God. Now it's quite possible that these plans for action will be thwarted. Peter intended to remain loyal to Jesus, yet in the crucial hour denied him. Paul states that he often finds himself doing the very evil which he abhors and not doing the good he desires to do. Despite the fact that their actual behavior was at odds with the intention, their predisposition to act shows Peter and Paul's overall favorable attitude toward God. Jesus' remarks about lust and anger in the Sermon on the Mount show that he regarded contemplated action as an important part of man's inner response.

We conclude, therefore, that a person's attitude toward God is made up of what he believes concerning him, how he feels about him, and what he intends to do toward him. It's hard to change another's attitude because a real opinion shift requires movement in all three areas. In the early part of this century, theological liberals stressed that society's salvation depended on Christian social action. They tried to influence this component of attitude, but relegated doctrinal belief to a minor role. In reaction to the liberal position, the fundamentalist movement arose. These conservatives equated personal salvation with right belief, while often minimizing the place of feeling. In the last decade the Jesus People and charismatic fellowships have stressed affinity of the heart as the sign of oneness with God.

If we can learn anything from history, it is that the present-day Christian persuader must be concerned equally with all three: cognitive belief, emotional affect, and behavioral intention. We ignore any of them to our own peril—and that of the gospel.

Drawing by Weber; © 1974 The New Yorker Magazine, Inc.

"That dog is their whole life."

* * * *

Attitudes can be displayed pictorially. It's common practice to sum up what a person believes, feels, and intends to do about a specific attitude object, and to represent this as a point on a favorable/unfavorable continuum. Take a look at the attitude scale below. From all that I've told you about my response to dogs, what point on the line best represents my attitude?

ATTITUDE TOWARD DOGS

Negative							Positive
−3	−2	−1	0	+1	+2	+3	

If I was rating myself, I think I'd place an X on the line somewhere between the +2 and +3. Let's face it—I like dogs. But somehow this one-dimensional scale is too simplistic. A realistic map of my attitude must not only show how positive or negative I am toward dogs, but must also portray another dimension—how *important* dogs are to me.

To me, a dog is a pet. Pets are nice, but there are a number of things which I value more highly. I'm more involved in God, my wife and children, our home, teaching, friends, my Young Life club, flying, our church, sports, and reading than I am in dogs. Contrast this with a man I know who is a bachelor. He breeds dogs for sale and show. As a sideline, he teaches dog obedience classes. For a vacation, he takes his dogs up into the north woods to hunt. In short, his whole life revolves around dogs. In comparison to him, I give dogs a rather low priority in my life. A two-dimensional attitude grid like the one below can depict not only my evaluation of an object, but also its overall centrality in my life. I've placed an X partway up on the right-hand side. This shows that I'm quite favorably disposed toward dogs, but that they are only moderately important in my life.

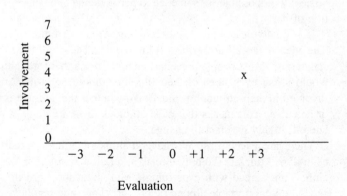

ATTITUDE TOWARD DOGS

INVOLVEMENT. The term "involvement" is used by one attitude researcher to designate membership in a group with a known stand. If I belonged to the Antivivisection League, which opposes medical experimentation on live dogs, he would consider me highly involved in my attitude. There are different terms to describe this second dimension of attitudes. Another researcher uses "saliency" as a test of importance. How often do I think about dogs? If I constantly daydream about dogs, they are salient. A third talks about "instrumentality." What does my attitude do for me? If appreciating dumb beasts makes me feel loving and worthwhile, my attitude has high instrumentality for me. Yet another speaks of "centrality." The closer my attitude toward dogs is to the person that I consider the real me, the greater its centrality. All of these terms zero in on the same idea. An attitude consists not only of a person's beliefs, feelings, and plans to act—it also reflects how important the whole area is in his life.

I've already suggested that attitudes are hard to change. We might symbolize a person's beliefs, feelings, and future plans with an anchor, since an anchor resists movement. If there is low involvement, saliency, instrumentality, or centrality, the anchor will be a small one. This means that although the attitude is fixed, it is at least susceptible to forces of change. If Bowser bites me, I may alter my opinion toward dogs. On the other hand, high involvement means that the anchor will be huge. My wife is of utmost importance to me. Therefore it's going to be next to impossible for someone to persuade me to change my evaluation of her.

It's equally difficult to influence many people's attitude toward God. The idea of an all-powerful, all-knowing, all-just, all-loving God is staggering. Most people are smart enough to see that true faith in God would affect every area of their life. For this reason, they are highly involved in their attitude toward God—whether that attitude is positive or negative. This means that most attitudes toward God are firmly anchored, highly resistant to change.

There are exceptions. Whenever I think of attitude importance or centrality, I think of Tommy Grejalva, a fellow in my first Young Life club. Tom agreed with everything I said about the Lord in my messages, felt comfortable around other Christians, and regularly attended church and Young Life. But the times I asked him what this all meant to him, he would merely shrug his shoulders and say, "Ain't no big thing." He was favorable toward the Lord, he just didn't think it was worth getting into a sweat over the whole matter.

Jesus thought it was. Throughout his ministry he emphasized that the kingdom of God should be the ultimate priority of our lives. He said, "Seek *first* the kingdom of God . . ." The parables of the priceless pearl and the unjust steward remind us that it's worth giving up everything else to attain eternal life. Jesus draws the lines of discipleship so as to exclude those who value comfort, family, or riches ahead of him.

THE TARGET. This, then, is our target as Christian persuaders. We must become "all things to all men that by all means" we might encourage others to make Jesus Christ more central in their life, while becoming more positive in their beliefs, feelings, and intended action toward him.

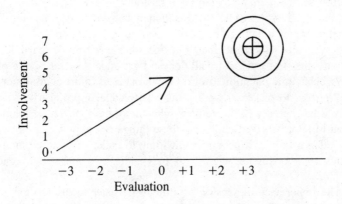

(Beliefs, Feelings, Intended Behavior)

How will we know when we've succeeded? How can we be sure that men have changed their attitude toward God? As stated in the introduction of this chapter, we can't! Unlike overt behavior, interior response cannot be directly observed. It's possible, however, to deduce some measure of attitude from a person's verbal and nonverbal communication. We can see into another "as through a glass darkly."

Beliefs are communicated verbally. The best way to find out what another person thinks is to ask him. We need to make certain, however, that we ask in a way that shows we really value his thoughts, instead of conducting a mini-heresy trial. If we create a judgmental atmosphere, he may tell us what he thinks we want to hear rather than what he really believes. Or he may remain mute!

Feelings are often communicated nonverbally. I recently heard a speaker begin his message with the words, "I'm really happy to be here." The agonized look on his face, his refusal to look at the audience, the shuffling of feet, the halting rate of the speech, and the flatness of his voice told us his real feelings. Facial expression, eye contact, body tension, and tone of voice are important clues as to what a person feels when he talks about God. But here again we must be careful not to assume that all positive or negative feelings are directed toward God. They may be emotional reactions to us.

Men are creatures of habit. Most human behavior is regularized. We eat three times a day, go to work at a set time, see friends somewhat systematically. It's a sad fact, but true, that if we don't schedule an activity ahead of time, it usually doesn't get done. We can spot a person's behavioral intention toward God through his future commitments. Willingness to make a monthly financial pledge, a promise to be involved in a weekly Bible study, a schedule of daily prayer, a commitment to tutor deprived children—these things reveal plans for positive Christian action. If a person is unwilling to make any future commitments for worship or witness, it may indicate a more unfavorable attitude.

The importance dimension of attitude is easier to discern than the three facets of the positive-negative dimensions just discussed. We can gauge the amount of a man's involvement in an area by the proportion of resources he voluntarily commits to it. By resources, I include:

Time—*If you care, you'll be there.*
Money—*If you want to know what is important to a man, look at his checkbook.*
Energy–*Sorry, honey; Daddy's too tired to play right now.*

This last week I went to three hockey games. My son is a goalie on the team. I attended a meeting for interested parents and watched parts of two games on TV. Including the time I spent buying tickets for a Chicago Blackhawk game, I spent nine and a half hours this week on hockey. The dollar cost for Jim's ice time and tickets to the Hawks game totaled $16.50. Energy-wise, I shivered through the three games that were played in unheated rinks. From the proportion of resources I invest in the sport, it's easy to spot my high involvement—I'm a hockey nut.

We can use the same criteria to gain a glimpse of God's centrality in a person's life. A few years ago, I spoke at a church retreat. On the bus ride home, a high school sophomore sat down next to me and told me he'd given his life to Jesus the night before. I was thrilled at his response, and proceeded to tell him of a discipleship group that would help him in his newfound faith. He was excited about this until he found it was on a Sunday night. At that point his face fell and he said he couldn't make it—"Gunsmoke" was on TV during that time.

Our target is attitude change, and attitudes toward God are hard to change. We've seen that it's not enough to concentrate just on a person's beliefs, or his feelings, or his plans to act. We must deal with all three, while at the same time encouraging him to let God have a greater priority in his life. The Christian advocate has a tough job. The enormity of the task has tempted some Christians to use questionable methods of persuasion. The next chapter considers the Christian's ethical responsibilities as he seeks to influence others for Jesus Christ.

An Ethic for the Christian Persuader

"I don't care what the method is as long as it brings people to Jesus Christ. If it works, it's OK. Being a Christian is so vastly more important than anything else that the end justifies almost any means."

The speaker was a graduate student in my Persuasion class. The discussion that day centered on the ethics of evangelism. In his statement, this fellow equated being effective with being ethical. He was echoing the feelings of many Christians who assume that any method of Christian influence is good if it has positive results. I challenge that assumption.

God has much to say about our attempts at influence apart from their success or failure. The entire second chapter of First Thessalonians is concerned with the ethics of persuasion. Specifically, Paul says:

For our appeal does not spring from error or uncleanness, nor is it made with guile; but just as we have been approved by God to be entrusted with the gospel, so we speak, not to please men, but to please God who tests our hearts. For we never used either words of flattery, as you know, or a cloak for greed, as God is witness; nor did we seek glory from men, whether from you or from others, though we might have made demands as apostles of Christ. But we were gentle among you, like a nurse taking care of her children. So being affectionately desirous of you, we were ready to share with you not only the gospel of God but also our own selves, because you had become very dear to us (1 Thessalonians 2:3-8).

I want to be careful not to overstate the distinction between moral methods of persuasion and effective ones. Obviously in God's eyes they are related. When Paul lays down the qualifications for effective leadership in the church, he stresses moral purity as the essential criterion (1 Timothy 3 and Titus 1). It's quite possible that in God's economy, being ethical and being effective are one and the same. The problem is, however, that due to our finite and sinful nature, we don't always have the mind of Christ as to when the results of our persuasion are positive. We're often satisfied when our influence occasions outward signs of devotion toward God. Then too, we're easily impressed by immediate results, whereas God not only takes the long-run view, he can also see the unintended side effects which we miss. Therefore we're on shaky ground when we try to defend the rightness of our methods with a clouded view of their results. As ambassadors for Christ, we need to have an ethical standard which guides our appeal regardless of how people respond.

I believe there is such a standard. Simply stated, it is this: *Any persuasive effort which restricts another's freedom to choose for or against Jesus Christ is wrong.*

We can see the validity of this standard by taking a look at the persuasive tactics which make us mad. In any such discussion, the term "manipulation" quickly arises. We don't like to be manipulated! While we may differ as to the specific techniques which arouse our judicial ire at being conned, had, suckered, etc., we find that in all of them, our free choice has been compromised. We've been manipulated and we don't like it. The Golden Rule says, "Do unto others as you would have them do unto you." Since we don't like others manipulating us, we must act so as not to remove free choice from them.

Some social scientists object to the idea that humans are free to choose. They claim that man is nothing but the result of biological, psychological, and sociological conditions, or the product of heredity and environment. Thus, B. F. Skinner holds that autonomous man is a

Handelsman

"Tell me more about this Christianity of yours. I'm terribly interested."

myth. All of man's so-called "decisions" are actually determined by previous experience. Even some Christians believe that all of men's actions are determined by God, and that they have no free choice.

Such a view of man must be met head-on. If free choice is a myth, so is moral obligation. C. S. Lewis notes that a deterministic view brings about the abolition of man. In an impassioned plea he argues that you cannot strip men of autonomy without denuding them of responsibility.

In a sort of ghastly simplicity we remove the organ and expect of them virtue and enterprise. We laugh at honour and are shocked to find traitors in our midst. We castrate and bid the geldings be fruitful.[1]

This is not to say that human choice is capricious or that there are no reasons for our decisions. I just received a phone call from a friend asking me to play tennis. I decided to stay in my office to write rather than go to the court—a rather uncharacteristic decision for me. A number of factors guided my choice—a love of tennis, enjoyment of competition, a feeling of guilt that this chapter is long overdue, a slightly twisted right knee, the knowledge that my wife is taking care of our kids so I can be free to write, etc. People who know me well might be able to predict my decisions with a high degree of accuracy. In this case my friend did! As he made his offer he said, "I know you'll probably end up deciding to write, but how 'bout . . ." Prediction, however, is not determinacy. Even though my behavior had recognizable parameters and even causes, I was able to select which factors would predominate. I can freely decide how I'll weight each variable, and whether I'll heed some and ignore others. Next time I may play tennis!

The writer of Proverbs speaks with wonder at the "way of a man with a maiden" (Proverbs 30:19). The image which comes to my mind is of the sincere lover tenderly wooing the affections of the undecided young girl. This is the ethical Christian persuader.* He lovingly pleads his case while carefully respecting the rights of his beloved. Note that he must always respect the other's right to freely choose, to say no. Jesus let the rich young ruler walk away.

Christian ethical thinkers have usually seen biblical ethics as involv-

---

*This is not a new concept. In the *Phaedrus*, Plato speaks of the rhetorician as lover. Kierkegaard uses the analogy to describe the Christian persuader in his *Philosophical Fragments*.

ing two requirements—love and justice. Love is concerned with the consequences of an act upon the other person. The loving persuader cares about the good or bad that comes from his influence. Because he cares about the other person as a person, he tries to figure out ahead of time what will happen as a result of his action in order that he might bring about the most good possible for the other. To answer the question, "What is the loving thing to do?" a persuader must make value judgments as to the relative worth of various results.

Justice is concerned with universal obligations—the oughts of life. The just persuader cares about the rightness or wrongness of his attempts of influence. "Is it ever right to lie?" or "Is it wrong to use emotional appeals?" are questions of justice. If we come to the conclusion that the end doesn't justify the means, we are doing so by an appeal to justice—not love. To answer the question, "What is the just thing to do?" a persuader must look to universal rules of conduct such as "Thou shalt not bear false witness."

The problem is, of course, that not all lovers are loving or just. There are false lovers as well as true lovers. I would like to use the analogy of the false lover to look at some typical ethical abuses in Christian persuasion. The diagram below charts the various types of lovers in regard to their concern for love and justice. As we look at each category of false lover, we will find that his shortcomings involve the removal of free choice to respond to Jesus Christ. This is immoral because true love is not coerced, it is freely given.

LOVE

	+	−	
+	True Lover	Legalistic Lover	
JUSTICE			Non-Lover
−	Smother Lover	Flirt Seducer Rapist	

THE NON-LOVER. The non-lover is he who does not try to per-suade. At first blush this looks like an attractive option, for the non-lover avoids all of the manipulative excesses entered into by the false lover. "Live and let live" is the non-lover's motto.

I do my thing, and you do your thing. I am not in this world to live up to your expectations, and you are not in this world to live up to mine. ("Gestalt Prayer," Fritz Perls)

The detached stance, however, is a luxury unavailable to the Christian. He takes seriously the right of each individual to choose, and he desires that God's way be a live option for every man. Without his persuasive effort, another might not be free to choose for Christ. He knows that no man is an island, and that to decide not to influence is to decide to let others' influence hold sway. The non-lover has opted out; he has left the field. He is perhaps more unethical than the false lover because he has shown that he doesn't care about his own beliefs or the other person.

Martin Luther King, Jr. promoted a 1965 human rights rally with the slogan, "If you care, you'll be there." This is God's message for the non-lover. In regard to Christian influence, it is better to have loved and lost than not to have loved at all. To those who are contemplating the possibility of being a non-persuader, Paul queries:

But how are men to call upon him in whom they have not believed? And how are they to believe in him of whom they have never heard? And how are they to hear without a (lover)? (Romans 10:14,15)

THE FLIRT. The flirtatious lover is not in love with another person. He is in love with himself, or in love with love. He is out to make as many conquests as he can. The Christian flirt is the evangelist who is more concerned about getting another scalp for his belt than he is for the welfare of his hearer. He sees people merely as souls. An emphasis on numbers often indicates a flirtatious tendency. The numbers may signify the great throng who attended a rally, the many souls won, or the multitude of followers collected by a charismatic leader. The 1974 International Congress on World Evangelization has confessed in its

Lausanne Covenant that evangelicals have "become unduly preoccupied with statistics." The emphasis here is on success and not on the person whom Christ calls us to serve.

We often smile at the puppy love antics of the flirt, but the injustice of his "love them and leave them" tactics can cause longlasting scars. The flirtatious Christian persuader lavishes attention upon a prospective convert until that individual makes a decision for Christ. Then, flushed with the success of obtaining a new trophy of grace, he moves on to new conquests, neglecting the one whom he so recently favored. This is immoral! Throughout his letters Paul stresses the importance of growing to maturity in Jesus Christ. He backed up these words by spending three months in Greece, eighteen months in Corinth, and over two years in Ephesus. When he was apart from them he wrote letters, sent other brethren, and remembered them in his prayers. The loving persuader will avoid the hit and run tactics of the flirt.

THE SEDUCER. The seducer uses deception and flattery to entice the other person into submission. He often appeals to irrelevant desires for success, money, popularity, or an easy life in order to accomplish his ends. He's willing to shade the truth because he fears that reality will put a damper on the other person's response.

The "testimony" has become a mainstay of Christian persuasion. The typical testimony is told by the successful businessman, beauty queen, or sports hero. The story line usually consists of how rotten things were, of becoming a Christian, and of how great things are now. This is devious because it suggests that all these good things will come to the listener if he turns to Jesus. It's similar to the deception of TV commercials which promise sex appeal from a toothpaste, popularity from a mouthwash, or the undying love of your husband if you serve the right brand of coffee.

The gospel does not promise these things. In fact, the weight of Scripture suggests that we shouldn't anticipate the world's honors and goods as a result of our faith. It's also unrealistic (and unjust) to promise that "Every day with Jesus is sweeter than the day before." Just once I'd like to hear a Christian testify that he'd been president of IBM, an Olympic medal winner, or a rock star, and that it had been great. He'd given his life to Christ and was trying to live up to the Lord's teachings.

As a result, he'd lost his money, fame, or ability and was now having a tough time—but that he praised the Lord anyhow.

The religious seducer is immoral because he maneuvers the listener into making a decision for the wrong reasons. He may do this by presenting only part of the gospel. Perhaps he portrays the strictness of God's law without stressing the love and forgiveness of Jesus Christ. Or he might emphasize the glories of personal salvation without mentioning the gospel's demands for social justice.

Another way to encourage the right decision for the wrong reason is to pair Christianity with something attractive to the listener. Americanism, the youth culture, or even the messenger himself have often been used to appeal to persons who would otherwise have no interest in being associated with the faith. This latter practice is one that deeply troubled Sören Kierkegaard. If the messenger is irresistibly attractive, others may respond to his winsome personality, not the gospel. This danger led Kierkegaard to advise that the Christian witness not try to persuade in the moral sense, but to merely explain the basics of the faith when asked—to give an account of the hope within.

Soliciting money can easily be the act of the seducer. A prime example of this could recently be seen in the movie *Marjoe*. The film showed the boy evangelist, Marjoe Gortner, presenting a Jesus that he himself denied, in order to collect money. There are less gross but equally disturbing examples among sincere Christians. I question the ethics of overcharging for the expenses of a Christian growth seminar and subsequently spending the excess money for a different purpose. The practice used by many radio ministers of offering special gifts to entice contributions seems equally seductive.

The Apostle Paul did not need to pander to people's baser desires, pretend that he was taking a survey, or in any other devious way sneak up on an unsuspecting "victim."

We use no hocus-pocus, no clever tricks, no dishonest manipulation of the Word of God. We speak the plain truth . . .For it is Christ Jesus as Lord whom we preach, not ourselves; we are your servants for Jesus' sake . . . This priceless treasure we hold, so to speak, in a common earthenware jar—to show that the splendid power of it belongs to God and not us. (2 Corinthians 4:2-7, *Phillips*)

"Would I lie to you?"

THE RAPIST. In our look at the unloving and unjust persuader we have seen first the flirt, then the seducer, and now finally the rapist. It does seem that there is an increasing disregard for the other person's free choice in these three types. The flirt is immature—we look on him with some pity. The seducer is immoral—we condemn him. The rapist is criminal—we remove him from society.

Rape is an act of force. There is no other term which so accurately describes some types of religious coercion. Before his conversion, Saul sought to drag Christians out of the Damascus synagogues in order to bring them back to Jerusalem (Acts 9:1). This sounds quite similar to the kidnapping activities of Ted Patrick, an evangelical minister. Patrick has physically abducted young men and women who had left their original biblical faith to join an autocratic cult or sect. Often with the encouragement and help of his parents, the victim has been held captive while he was "deprogrammed." One gets the disconcerting impression that many Christians would use force to impose their will if only they were part of a powerful ruling majority. The history of torture perpetuated by the Jesuit missionaries and the whole Inquisition are cases in point.

Force can be psychological as well as physical. Any time one "makes you an offer you couldn't refuse," it's rape. Highly charged emotional situations fit this category, for they render the participant virtually helpless to resist the suggestion of the leader. There is nothing wrong with emotion. God made us emotional beings and personal involvement is a vital part of apprehending truth. But crowded revivals singing seventeen choruses of "Just As I Am" or late night campfire say-so meetings can remove the element of conscious choice.

I believe that there's a special danger inherent for those who work with kids. Historically, many Christian clubs and camps have used high pressure tactics to obtain a decision for Christ. The average preadolescent is not equipped to withstand the positive incentive of counselor approval or the negative force of group condemnation. The phrase "age of consent" in our legal code points to the fact that children may be unable to say no to the forceful persuader. Jesus made it clear that leading a child astray is a particularly heinous act. I think this applies to the methods used as well as the intended results.

Probably the most widespread persuasive tactic used in the church is

"If only there were a way I could force them to love me."

guilt. Undoubtedly this is due to the fact that it's so easy to make people feel guilty if they don't teach a Sunday school class, serve on a committee, tithe, witness for Christ, or you name it. Those who are somewhat insensitive won't cave in under the pressure, but will feel bad and unworthy. Those with more acute consciences will be unable to withstand the pangs. They'll end up doing something they would have otherwise rejected, accompanied by a gnawing bitterness at being had. Either way it's rape.

THE SMOTHER LOVER. The smother lover loves you to death. He loves you so much that he won't take no for an answer. We often think of unrequited love as an act of beauty and devotion, but his persistence in the face of a clear-cut rejection is unjust and can be downright obnoxious.

The smotherer's injustice lies in his refusal to respect the free choice of another human. I once heard a personal evangelist who said he started out every conversation on an airplane with the question, "Are you interested in spiritual things?" Usually the other person would respond with a somewhat tentative yes, and the evangelist would feel free to go into his planned presentation. If the other person said no, however, the evangelist was undaunted. He'd say, "That's strange. Most people are. Here's the reason why . . ." and he'd be off on the same thirty-minute presentation as before. Recently the U.S. Supreme Court ruled that citizens have the civil right to freedom from invasion of privacy. As Christians we should grant a similar right to those who have indicated that they couldn't care less about our faith.

A Christian leader will often smother his followers by not giving them enough room to breathe. By this I mean a pattern of paternalistic rules and regulations which reflect the leader's conviction that he knows what's best. His love for his people is genuine, but he's afraid they'll go astray, so he lays down one set program for maturing in the faith. He often tries to limit them from hearing other points of view.

This unitary approach to discipleship fails to take into account the vast differences of personality and needs among people. It is unjust because it treats everyone identically, ignoring the uniqueness of each human being. Theologian Harvey Cox is severely critical of religious persuasion which involves only one-way communication.

One-way "communication" by decree, fiat or promulgation is viewed by the Bible as the style not of prophets but of tyrants and oppressors. In the New Testament the apostles speak in synagogues and public places. They expose themselves to danger and rejection as well as to authentic acceptance.[2]

He asserts that every man needs to tell his individual story of response to God. Videotaped lectures, radio-TV broadcasts, or any other impersonal means which leave no room for spontaneous effective response can be dehumanizing.

The smotherer means well. But can we ethically justify our actions on the basis of good intentions? To some extent, yes. The other day my son, Jim, climbed into my lap while I was watching TV. In the process he placed his knee painfully in my stomach. As I groaned he said, "Sorry, Dad, I didn't mean to." I knew that, and the physical hurt was more than offset by my pleasure at his desire to cuddle together. But suppose he did it again fifteen minutes later, and again after that? I think that I'd be justifiably vexed at his casual unconcern for my welfare.

This illustrates the moral obligation which we have as Christian persuaders to monitor the actual consequences of our actions. I believe that the more we limit the choice of another person, the greater the responsibility we must bear for his life. James warns us, "Let not many of you become teachers, my brethren, for you know that we who teach shall be judged with greater strictness" (James 3:1).

THE LEGALISTIC LOVER. "If I speak in the tongues of men and of angels, but have not love, I am a noisy gong or a clanging cymbal" (1 Corinthians 13:1). The legalistic lover lacks love. He persuades purely out of a sense of obligation or duty. He is the preacher who presents the weekly altar call even though there's not an unbeliever in the congregation. He is the feeble-hearted lover, and others can spot that he's only going through the motions. The legalistic lover is an ineffective persuader, but more to the point of this chapter, the legalist is unethical.

In his classic book *I and Thou*, Martin Buber stresses the immorality of treating a person as only a means to an end—a thing or an it. Buber reminds us that it is not enough just to love God. We must love man as well. He claims that whoever knows the world as something to be utilized knows God the same way.

The legalistic persuader refuses to look at the total needs of man. While presenting the words of personal salvation, he chooses to ignore the very real human needs for food, peace, dignity, or accomplishment. James has a scathing denunciation of such loveless persuasion.

If a fellow man or woman has no clothes to wear and nothing to eat, and one of you say, "Good luck to you. I hope you'll keep warm and find enough to eat," and yet give them nothing to meet their physical needs, what on earth is the good of that? (James 2:15, 16, *Phillips*)

THE TRUE LOVER. The true lover is he who is both loving and just. He is the persuader who cares more about the welfare of the other person than he does about his own ego. He makes his appeal in a manner that respects the human rights of other people. Although saddened, he's willing to let the other person say no. The New Testament presents a picture of Paul as the true lover.

It's hard to cite a contemporary example who fulfills all the requirements of the true lover. I must confess that I spot myself more easily in the false lover categories than in this one. I have flirted with other people's affections, being more concerned that they succumb to the faith than I was in providing longlasting nurture. I have allowed them to be seduced into believing that becoming a Christian will make them popular. Nor is rape a stranger. I have at times played to the emotions of others to the point where I doubt their ability to think clearly. I've smothered people by accepting only a specific word formula as evidence of their faith, and I have at times shown such a legalistic lack of love for another that I would witness to him without even bothering to learn his name.

Thank God that he is willing to forgive me for this unethical behavior—and all others like myself. He may even have used our actions to further his will. But this is no excuse for us to continue immoral practices. We can use our Lord Jesus Christ as a model of what our behavior should be. I'm impressed by the beautiful mix of justice and love which he achieved with the Samaritan woman at the well (John 4). He justly told her the truth about her errors in morals and theology, but he did so in a loving way which spared her needless embarrassment. Notice that he seems to have sent the disciples away to get food so that he could be alone to talk with her. It's doubtful that such a personal conversation would have taken place in a crowd. It's probably the only time in history that twelve people went to get food for thirteen—or fourteen, for surely Jesus would have met her physical needs as well.

Christ shows the same regard for people in other encounters recorded in John's Gospel. He is willing to see Nicodemus at night so as not to compromise his standing among the Pharisees. He carefully avoids causing further embarrassment to the woman taken in adultery, yet plainly tells her, "Do not sin again." He is responsive to the human needs of the wedding couple at Cana, the man born blind, the hungry multitudes, and the doubting Thomas. He is even willing for many of his disciples to leave him when he is motivated out of real love for the other person and his actions toward him are just. He is truly ethical in his appeal, and strikingly effective. God will use the moral man.

This then is the Christian ethic of persuasion. We must act so as to fulfill the requirement of love and the obligation of justice in seeking to guarantee the human freedom to choose toward God and man. This is a hard standard. But then Christ never promised that being faithful to the gospel would be easy.

MELT

4

Resistance to Persuasion

Back in the days of Socrates and Aristotle there was a group of Greek men called sophists. These were the professional persuaders of their time. They were mouths for hire—paid to deliver speeches for various causes. Although they were in great demand by the public, Plato holds them up to ridicule. He claims they were more interested in swaying men's minds than they were in truth.

The professional persuaders of our age have a similar image problem. Our language is laced with negative references to those whose job it is to influence. We speak of tricky lawyers, shifty politicians, slick Madison Avenue ad types, pushy salesmen, and windbag evangelists. Likewise the content of a persuasive message is often labeled manipulation, mere rhetoric, empty words, or propaganda.

Perhaps this isn't you. When you meet someone who's trying to get you to change, maybe you immediately jump up and say, "Hot dog! Boy, I'm glad this guy is trying to talk me into changing my mind." But if this is your reaction, you're part of a small minority. I know that *my* reaction is one of immediate resistance. As soon as someone suggests that I alter my way of life, I start thinking of counterarguments to oppose his pitch. The harder he pushes, the stronger I resist.

Why? Why do we resent efforts to persuade us? Is it just the sheer cussedness of man, or are there some valid reasons for our resistance? I can think of at least three such reasons—any one of which would make us wary of people trying to influence us.

LACK OF SINCERITY. One obvious reason we distrust the persuader is that we question his motives. Why is he doing this? What's in it for him? Does he really care about me as a person? These nagging questions occur to us whenever we're aware that someone wants us to change. We suspect an ulterior motive and we're put on our guard. For this reason, influence is often most effective when it's least obvious. If we know someone is trying to sway our beliefs, we'll raise barriers and won't deal with what he has to say. If, on the other hand, he has no apparent ax to grind, we'll often consider his way of thinking as a valid option for our own lives.

I recently met a girl who accepted the faith after overhearing Christians talk to each other about the Lord. She'd often heard the gospel, but always figured that Christians were a bunch of phonies. She reacted violently at any mention of the name Jesus Christ. Then she came to stay in the home of her aunt and uncle for a month during the summer. Many nights she lay awake overhearing them talk about their love of God and desire to serve him. Their obvious sincerity won her over. Imagine their surprise—and of course their joy—when she announced at the end of her stay that she wanted to be a Christian like them. It would've been a different story if they'd been constantly angling to convince her. Overt witness would have scared her off.

I'm not advocating that we go underground and pretend we don't care about another person's beliefs. What I am suggesting is that we lead transparent lives so that our motives are open for all to see. As the Apostle John put it: "We must write and tell you about it, because the more that fellowship extends the greater the joy it brings to us who are already in it."

We also need to make sure that our friendship with others isn't based on their coming over to our way of thinking. True love doesn't have strings attached. If we really care about others we'll continue to appreciate them even if they don't respond to our message.

I'D RATHER FIGHT THAN SWITCH. No one likes being wrong.

"Kids, here I am, all hooked up to this lie detector, ready to tell you all about Zapples, the exciting new breakfast cereal...."

It's even worse to have someone *tell* us we're wrong. Yet that's what we usually do when we try to convert someone to our lifestyle. Either directly or by implication, we make it clear that his thoughts are erroneous, his affections misplaced, and his actions inadequate. This· is a threatening sort of thing to hear. The fellow we're talking to has to live with himself twenty-four hours a day, and one of the ways he does this is to turn off or actively reject any message which implies he is wrong and needs to change. "Don't confuse me with the facts, my mind's made up."

Some early studies concerned with prejudice show that we're quite capable of reordering our perceptions of the world around us in order to maintain our conviction that we're right.[3] A group of white, middle-class New York City residents were presented with a picture of people on a subway. Two men were in the foreground. One was white, one was black. One wore a business suit, one was clothed in workman's overalls. One was giving his money to the other who was threatening him with a knife. Now as a matter of fact it was the black man who wore the suit, and it was he who was being robbed by the white laborer. But such a picture didn't square with the prejudices of the viewers. To them, white men were executives, black men were blue collar workers. Blacks were the robbers, whites the victims. And so they reported what their mind told them they saw—that a black laborer was assaulting a white businessman. As human beings who desperately desire our lives to be consistent and untroubled, we'll go to great lengths to reject a message that implies we're wrong.

It's so easy to adopt an attitude which shouts, "Everybody is wrong but me and thee—and sometimes I wonder about thee!" This just makes others more rigid in their already fixed positions. Paul avoided this trap when he addressed the men of Athens. Although he was tremendously vexed by the idolatry he saw, he didn't come on like gangbusters, hitting them over the head with their own sin. Instead he spoke well within their latitude of acceptance.

"Gentlemen of Athens, my own eyes tell me that you are in all respects an extremely religious people. For as I made my way here and looked at your shrines I noticed one altar on which were inscribed the words, TO GOD THE UNKNOWN. It is this God whom you are worshipping in ignorance that I am here to proclaim to you!" (Act 17:22, 23, *Phillips*)

Some of the audience laughed outright when he finished, but a few believed and many said they'd like to hear more. By respecting them as human beings, Paul overcame their natural reactance and won a sympathetic hearing for the gospel.

This is a hard lesson for me to learn. I'm afraid that I tend to be a judgmental person. It's so easy for me to criticize others in an attempt to look good. Jesus was right. I peek around the plank that protrudes out of my own eye in order to notice the speck of sawdust which bothers another. This is not only hypocritical. It also makes me forfeit the opportunity of influencing anyone I judge. As Christian persuaders, we need to bend over backwards to make sure that our attempts to influence others are not viewed as a knock of who they are.

DON'T FENCE ME IN. Have you ever noticed that we often want the very thing we can't have? Our cultural truisms reflect this fact: "Forbidden fruit tastes best." "The grass looks greener on the other side of the fence." And the bittersweet jest, "Why is it that everything I want is either illegal, immoral, or fattening?" I find this true in my own experience. I sit down in a restaurant, look at the menu, and decide I'll have the chicken. The waitress appears, but before she takes my order she announces that they're out of shrimp. All of a sudden I develop a craving for seafood.

There's a theory which explains our special desire for that which is moved from our reach.[4] It's called "psychological reactance." The theory is based on the idea of free choice. It suggests that there's a whole range of free behavior that is open to us in life. If another person takes away some of our options, we'll react. Those lost alternatives will become more attractive and we'll try to reestablish our right to do them. The greater the proportion of free behavior that's eliminated, the greater the amount of reactance we'll feel. We don't even have to actually lose the opportunity of doing something before we get stirred up. The mere threat or possibility that an option *might* be lost is enough to make us react. Let me give an example.

For many years the faculty members at my college have been offered two free lunches a week in the dining hall. The idea has been to encourage better professor-student relationships as we mingle and talk over the meal. Until recently I haven't taken full advantage of the opportunity. It's not that I don't like students. I've just tended to skip lunch and use the time for writing and working out at the local "Y." But then the business manager issued a warning that due to the lack of funds they might have to cut down on the complimentary meals. I reacted against this possible loss of benefits—even though I hadn't eaten that much of the free food. I suddenly found myself acting to reestablish my "right" to those student lunches. I now eat in the dining hall regularly twice a week.

What's all this have to do with resistance to persuasion? Just this—

many people regard any effort at persuasion as an attempt to box them in. They feel that this is an impingement on their freedom and react negatively toward the person who tries to proscribe their actions or beliefs. I think almost all of us tense up when confronted by the fast-talking, high-pressure salesman who counters our every attempt to say no with a new pitch. "What? You sez you ain't satisfied? You sez you want a better deal? I'll tell you what I'm gonna do . . ." We're repelled by such attempts to force our decision. The harder we're pushed, the more we resist.

There's a good chance that at sometime or other you've been visited by a caller from Jehovah's Witnesses. If you're like me, you've been impressed with the sincerity and conviction of these proselytes. But there's an inflexibility in their mood and manner that puts me off. It seems they have an automatic answer regardless of how I respond to their canned presentation. The relentless progression of proof texts goes on, no matter what.

This unitary approach does have its advantages. It steels the witness against any possible doubt which might be raised by the potential convert. It gains attention, and it may win over those who enjoy being dominated. But the vast majority of us become defensive when the other guy claims his belief is the only legitimate option. Instead of being drawn in, we're scared off.

There's a message here for the Christian advocate. We know that we have God's truth. John 14:6 assures us that Jesus is the only way to God—that the sole way to approach the Father is through him. But if the first thing a non-Christian hears about the faith is that there's only one way to believe, he probably won't stay around to comprehend our truth. It's much more effective to "give an account of the hope within us." Sharing how we've experienced God won't raise barriers in other people. Telling them how they should experience him will.

Please don't misinterpret what I'm saying. I'm not suggesting that we pretend that all roads lead to God or that every fuzzy thought about Jesus is correct. Rather it's a matter of stress. If we go forth with an upraised index finger boldly shouting "One Way!" most nonbelievers will experience psychological reactance. They'll be repelled before they have a chance to discover what that way is. If on the other hand we can gently nudge others to take a sympathetic look at our risen Savior, he'll draw men to himself. To put it bluntly: The hard sell is out!

Put these three factors together—a suspicion of our motives, a distaste at the idea of being wrong, and a fear of being pushed into a corner. Now you can readily see why we can't walk up to someone cold turkey and win them over to our cause. They must be melted first. I've already suggested a number of ways to start the thawing process. Be human. Be transparent. Act without guile. Nudge, don't judge. I doubt if a Christian has ever argued someone into the kingdom. Be willing to admit you don't have a monopoly on the truth.

All of this reflects an attitude that is summed up in the title of a vintage Pat Boone popular song—"Friendly Persuasion." It goes along with another melting approach I presented in Chapter 1—being sensitive enough to be able to spot those times in his life when he's open to your message. And it's certainly consistent with the ethics of respecting another's free choice outlined in the previous chapter.

I hope you can tell by this time that I'm firmly convinced an honest love and concern for the other person is the best way to overcome his natural wariness. There are, however, some additional persuasive appeals and techniques which have traditionally been used to diminish resistance to influence. Three of these—guilt, fear, and role play—will be considered in depth in following chapters. But first I want to touch briefly upon three others.

DISTRACTION. Public speakers hate distractions. Every speaker has a pet list of disturbances which cut into his hearers' concentration. For me, babies crying, people whispering in the back row, police sirens, and open copies of *TIME* are among the most irritating. I intuitively feel that I'm more persuasive when I have the undivided attention of my audience, and anything which breaks the concentration strikes me as bad. But my gut feeling may be wrong! Research shows that rather than being a hindrance, some forms of distraction can actually aid persuasion.

We've already seen that people don't like to be persuaded. When they become aware that someone is trying to move them, they toss up filters to screen out unwanted ideas. If they hear a discrepant message, they'll mentally say "Yes, but . . ." and begin to think up counterarguments. But distractions can nullify the problem. If the listener doesn't focus on the message, he may not realize the speaker's persuasive intent. Even if he's aware that his position is challenged, he may not have time to counterargue. It's as if the new message has a direct pipeline into his mind, unimpeded by filters, screens, or barricades.

Does this really work? In some cases it does. In one study, college men saw a movie knocking Greek letter fraternities.[5] Fraternity members who viewed the film without any distractions remained unmoved. It attacked their lifestyle and they resisted. Other fraternity men heard the same anti-Greek sound track, but were distracted by the pictures on the screen. Instead of seeing the man who delivered the speech, they saw a completely unrelated humorous short. They had to split their attention between the audio and the visual presentations. These fellows ended up much more convinced than those who could concentrate solely on the persuasive message.

Distraction doesn't always work. It's possible to have interference so great that the listener can't even grasp the main point of the message. Obviously this won't help your cause. Usually a mild diversion is better than a strong one.

It's also been found that a pleasurable distraction will facilitate change more than an irritating one. Occasionally my wife reads to me while giving me a back rub. The enjoyment is great and my mind is only half on the words she's reading. But strangely enough I almost always seem to agree with the thrust of the article.

This isn't to suggest that back rubs become a staple of every Bible study or worship service—although the human warmth that can be conveyed by touch might go a long way to disarm those who are wary around Christian things. What it does suggest is that a continually changing multimedia show can be more effective than a straight sermon as a means of getting an audience to honestly consider new ideas. A list of other pleasant distractions might include background organ music during a church offering, a cup of hot coffee at a discussion group, or the presence of close friends at a meeting.

The idea of a Christian leader sitting down and coldly planning out a series of pleasant distractions strikes me as somewhat sinister. I don't recommend it. But I do think we need to see that some distractions may help as much as hinder our cause. This knowledge will keep us from getting uptight if it looks as though not everyone is paying attention to us.

HUMOR. If you judge only by the results of laboratory research, you quickly conclude that humor is a lousy persuasive approach. Most studies fail to find any advantage when humor is part of the message. In fact, humor seems to have some striking drawbacks.

In the first place, it's hard to be genuinely funny. Most of us aren't Bill Cosbys, Bob Newharts, or Woody Allens—nor do we have high-paid joke writers backing us up. It's downright painful for an audience when humor bombs. We're not grateful to the speaker who makes us sit and squirm while he desperately gropes for a laugh. When humor falls flat it sets our teeth on edge and we more readily oppose the speaker's ideas.

Of course we sometimes may miss his comic intention. In this case the results are diametrically opposed to what he intended. I've seen this happen with Joe Bayly's *The Gospel Blimp*. To me, the book is the funniest piece of Christian satire I've read. It's the tale of two families who want to reach their neighbors for Christ, so they buy a blimp to tow banners and drop tracts over their homes. The story is a clever parody of impersonal methods of evangelism—a classic study of how *not* to do it. Yet I know of people who've read the book and missed the irony. They thought a blimp was a great evangelistic idea and wanted to get one for their own community.

Even if the audience catches the humorous intent and finds the words amusing, there's still a danger that the comic material will cloud the thrust of the message to such an extent that they'll miss the main point. There's a speaker who comes periodically to Wheaton College's chapel. The students always look forward to his message because of his tremendous sense of humor. He leaves them rolling in the aisles. But the man has a problem. Although his listeners acclaim him as an entertaining speaker, they seldom remember what he said. His jokes obscure the serious part of his message.

A final problem with humor is that it can be quite cutting. Sit down and analyze a batch of funny cartoons. You'll find that 90 percent describe basically unfunny or even tragic situations—happening to someone else. Almost every joke pokes fun at a class of people or ideas. If

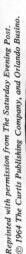

"Well, so much for satire."

the butt of the humor is held near and dear by part of the audience, the humor backfires and people are turned off.

Having said all this, it may come as a surprise when I say that humor is a great way to overcome resistance to persuasion. Why am I willing to maintain this belief in the face of contrary experimental evidence? Because I've heard black comedian Dick Gregory speak before 2000 hostile students at the University of Alabama and within an hour have them considering liberal ideas that they'd reject out of hand in another situation. Because I recall John F. Kennedy disarming cynical reporters with a well-placed quip. Because I've seen Bruce Larson of Faith at

Work use humor to bring a tightly Calvinistic audience to a sympathetic understanding of relational theology. Because I was part of a lethargic chapel congregation that came to life at the British wit of the Rev. Stuart Briscoe. And finally, I believe in the power of humor to influence because I've seen it work in my own ministry.

If humor is as effective as I claim it to be, why haven't researchers spotted this in controlled laboratory studies? It may be that experimental social scientists have a tough time being humorous, and people who are naturally funny aren't attracted to rigorous scientific research— seriously! Valid humor research needs both qualities, and the combination is rare. The problem may also be that most persuasion research has been run on an artificial "one-shot" basis. Humor's effectiveness might well be greatest in a real-life situation when a speaker has repeated exposures to the same audience as in a weekly church service or college classroom.

Comic material is a great attention getter. We hear such a glut of persuasive messages that we're apt to let them roll over us without absorbing what's said. A well-timed joke or an ironic observation will arrest our attention long enough to pick up the actual message. Increased credibility is another factor. We're suspicious of the "all business" type who comes on like Scrooge or a Grinch. It's easier to trust the fellow who doesn't appear to take himself quite so seriously. *Hum*or makes us *hum*an.

There are plenty of reasons to believe that humor should be a positive melting agent in persuasion. And in line with what I presented in the last section, humor is a pleasant distraction. Laughter can keep us from noticing the persuasive intent of a speaker and it can sidetrack us from our usual practice of counterarguing a new idea.

It's much easier to figure out why humor is effective than it is to give direct advice on how to be funny. To a large extent it's a matter of personality. Some people could draw laughter reading names from the phone book, while others would have a tough time getting a rise using a bushel basket of time-proven jokes. I know of only one path everyone can travel that guarantees lots of warm laughter from an audience. That route is to laugh at yourself.

I've already stated that most humor involves something unfunny happening to someone else. You are someone else. If you're willing to share embarrassing or painful experiences and show that you reacted in an ignorant, ridiculous, or even dumb manner, others will feel free to laugh with you. This is the essence of Bill Cosby's humor. He tells about incongruous things that happened to him as he grew up, and then lets the audience know that he realizes he looked stupid. This gives them permission to laugh—and they roar. We can do it just as well as Cosby if we don't take ourselves too seriously. That's not always easy. As Christians who know the purpose of life, seeking to redeem the time, desirous of others coming to know the Lord, we can slip into a determined grimness. But if we can begin to come up with a wry appreciation of human foibles—our own as well as others—we'll be one step ahead in making others laugh.

So I highly recommend that we be willing to laugh at ourselves and let others join in the hilarity. It will keep us from being too pompous. And it will give them the chance to examine the deep-felt convictions without having to first climb over a mountain of doubts and suspicions. Humor melts resistance to persuasion.

CROWDING. Distraction and humor are persuasive techniques that can be used equally well in a one-on-one situation or with a large group. There's another melting strategy that depends on the presence of a number of people—crowding. For many years public speakers have felt intuitively that they were more effective when the audience was packed in. It isn't so much the size of the crowd that's important, but rather how tightly the people are jammed together. Aides of the late Senator Robert Kennedy told supporters at Northwestern that it's better to have a full room of 100 people than the Hollywood Bowl with 100 empty seats. During the restoration of the House of Commons after World War II, Winston Churchill ruled that the building should be maintained intentionally small so that it would accommodate only two-thirds of the members of Parliament. He argued that it was better to crowd in more than the Chamber could comfortably seat than to have the possibility of empty benches. Hitler and Mussolini intentionally crowded their audiences together because they believed that such audiences were more easily persuaded.

I've always been interested in the possible connection between crowding and persuasion. When I was on Young Life staff, it was standard procedure to line up homes that were small enough to insure that the living room would be full. Somehow this made for an atmosphere of excitement which helped overcome the doubts and fears of newcomers. Despite my conviction that crowding enhanced persuasion, I could never find any research establishing the connection. I decided to investigate this myself.[6]

I used a small classroom for the experiment. The 17x18-foot room contained thirty movable chairs. I found a doctor who was willing to deliver a fifteen-minute speech opposing medical experimentation on live animals. I picked antivivisection as a topic because most people don't have deep-seated convictions on the issue. I wanted to see if those who heard the plea in a crowded room would shift their opinions more than those who listened as part of a sparse audience.

The physician gave the speech in four different audience situations. I call them scattered, full, packed, and jammed. In the scattered condition, the audience consisted of only fifteen people. They were spread around the room, and the empty seats were obvious to all comers. Each of the thirty seats was filled in the full condition. The packed situation was definitely crowded. Forty-five people heard the speech in the same small room. Some were seated, others stood around the back of the room, and a few sat on the carpet right in front of the speaker. People were really squeezed together in the jammed condition. There were sixty bodies trying to occupy a space made for half that number. Some who were seated held others on their laps. Those standing were pressed tightly against each other. It's hard to imagine a more crowded audience.

Each participant filled out attitude surveys before and after the speech. The results showed that crowding did indeed make a difference in persuasion. The listeners in the full, packed, and jammed audience were swayed more by the speech than those in the scattered condition. The difference was large enough so that it can't be passed off as mere chance. While the difference among the three most crowded situations wasn't that great, those who were part of the jammed audience were influenced the most.

I had set out to see if crowding facilitates persuasion. As it turned out, it does. But I also wanted to figure out why. I checked out a number of separate possibilities in the study, but had to discard all but one. That explanation was heightened emotion.

I used a paper and pencil test to determine emotional stress right after the speech. This test measures physical arousal consistent with such indicators as heartbeat, the amount of sweat on the palms, and pupil dilation. I found an almost one-on-one relationship between audience density and auditor arousal. The greater the crowding, the higher the emotional excitement. This in turn seems to render the hearer more susceptible to whatever persuasive appeal he hears.

I wasn't surprised that emotion proved to be a factor in persuasion. Down through the ages, radical personality change has always been associated with extreme emotional excitement. A brief scan of William James' *Varieties of Religious Experience* or any history of revivalism shows that this is true in the field of religion. The records of Hitler, Mussolini, Stalin, and modern Chinese inquisitors reveal that inner tension is a prerequisite for political brainwashing. Psychoanalytic literature from Freud on down claims that physical and mental stress can act as a necessary catalyst for successful therapy. But as you'll recall from the previous chapter on ethics, I'm quite leery of whipping up an emotional response to such an extent that a person loses his ability to freely choose.

Does the level of arousal found in the crowding study reach that critical point? I don't think so. The scattered audience appeared dead and listless. There was no emotion—no motion. Each individual sat alone and aloof, mentally resisting each argument. The more crowded listeners felt sufficient emotion to melt their resistance. They were drawn into the situation enough to actually hear and consider the message. I could see this in their visual reaction to the speech. When the room was at least full, the audience laughed at the jokes, winced at a gory example, and in general responded to the ideas that were presented. The jammed listeners actually applauded at the end of the speech. This was in sharp contrast to the scattered auditors who gave no visible response.

We've found that crowding has had a beneficial effect at our church. There's a chapel that seats 200 comfortably and a sanctuary that holds 400. Since the average attendance has traditionally been about 250 at the two Sunday morning worship services, both were held in the sanctuary. My pastor decided to switch the early service to the chapel. Immediately there was a certain spirit of excitement not found at the later worship. This atmosphere has attracted new members from the community to the point where 300 people now jam into the small chapel each week. Some members say that it's become so crowded that we should switch back to the larger sanctuary. Having an intuitive grasp of crowd psychology and knowing the results of my experiment, my friend and pastor just smiles and says he thinks he'll keep it the way it is.

*   *   *   *

In this chapter we've seen that psychological reactance is a fact of life. For a variety of reasons, people resist persuasion. They'll rebuff attempts to influence them unless they first experience a melting or thawing. I've suggested that this is most likely to happen when we show a genuine warmth and concern for others and don't get uptight in defending the rightness of our cause. In addition, there are a number of persuasive techniques which can aid in overcoming resistance to influence. We've looked briefly at distraction, humor, and crowding. We're now ready to consider major approaches to melting—guilt, fear, and role play.

61 ▷

5

Guilt*

The telephone rings. It's the lady who lives next door. "Is anybody missing from your home?" she asks. Immediately I feel a surge of guilt. Our basset hound has slipped out of the yard again and headed straight to her house. She thinks that we don't take good care of our dog, so she scolds us to make us be more responsible.

Our neighbor's persuasive tactics are not unique. Most of us use guilt as a device to get others to do what we want. This last week I told a college student that I was disappointed in his paper—he should do better. I criticized my son for leaving his baseball glove at the park— doesn't he know the value of money? I pointed out to a high school girl that she has ignored God for most of her life. Let's face it—these were attempts to make people feel bad so they'd change their attitudes and behavior.

I have just read over these words and must admit that I don't like the sound of them. Who am I to want to make people feel so bad? I search my mind for a way to justify what I have done. Perhaps the good which results from the use of guilt will far outweigh the person's discomfort.

*A portion of this chapter was originally published as an article in the Crawford Broadcasting Company Program Guide, Fall, 1973.

The student will learn more. Jim will take better care of his possessions. The girl will become a Christian.

But none of these results is certain. How effective is guilt as a means of persuasion? Specifically, is it wise to use guilt as a way to bring people closer to God?

There has been a considerable amount of experimental research concerning guilt in the last few years.[7] Suppose you volunteered to be a subject in such a study. What would happen? Well, in the first place you'd come to the experimental room without knowing the purpose of the research. You'd walk in and discover another person—we'll call him Pete—strapped into a heavy chair with electrodes attached to his arms and legs. The experimenter explains that the study has to do with the effects of punishment on learning. You are to be the teacher, Pete will be the learner. Your job is to teach Pete to memorize a series of ten-digit numbers. Whenever Pete makes a mistake, you are to punish him by pressing a button which gives him a painful 250-volt shock.

Now actually Pete won't feel a thing. He's a confederate of the experimenter who's been instructed to goof up some of the numbers and then pretend to feel pain when you push the button. Of course you don't know this. You think you're really hurting the guy. All this has been arranged to produce a feeling of guilt. The question is: Are you more susceptible to influence when you feel guilty than when you don't? Is guilt a powerful motivator?

The answer is Yes. After the session is over, Pete works it so that you leave the building together. He casually mentions that he's a Red Cross volunteer and has fifty phone calls to make that night asking for contributions. He wonders if you would be willing to make some of these calls.

Let's face it. These kinds of calls are no fun and they take a lot of time. Under most other circumstances you'd find some excuse, beg off, and refuse to help him. But if you're like the others who've taken part in the study, you'd feel bad that you hurt Pete and look for a way of getting rid of that guilt. The average experimental subject ends up agreeing to make twenty to thirty calls.

The research shows, therefore, that guilt is a powerful tool to get people to do what they wouldn't do normally. Before we rush off to use guilt as a technique to win people to Jesus Christ, however, we need to see the long-term effects of the tactic. As it turns out, persuasion through guilt has some potent side effects which can harm the cause of Christ.

The first of these side effects is avoidance. When someone makes us feel guilty, we try to avoid them in the future. This usually happens in the type of guilt research I've just described. Although you might do what Pete asked that one time, you'd gladly skip the opportunity of running into him again. I've had this happen to me.

I took about fifty non-Christian high school students on a skiing trip a few months ago. They all had come regularly to our weekly Young Life club. The second night twelve of the guys were walking along the main street of the ski village toward the lodge. I had previously asked them not to throw snowballs in town, but of course they did. One hit a passing car and cracked the windshield. Apparently the driver slammed on his brakes and jumped out of the car. He was extremely angry and called for the leader of the group. As soon as I arrived on the scene, he vented his wrath on me.

All of the guys felt very ashamed that they had gotten me in trouble. As one fellow put it, "Boy, do we feel bad. We'll pay for the damage. Anything we can do to help make it up to you, Em, let us know." This seemed to be a golden opportunity to begin influencing them for the cause of Christ, but it didn't turn out that way. Although they paid for the window, they still feel guilty toward me. Nine out of the twelve have never returned to the club.

So we see that guilt leads to avoidance. This has some frightening implications for the Christian persuader. Traditionally, our techniques of evangelism and discipleship have involved getting people to feel guilty about their conduct towards God. What we may be doing is guaranteeing that they will avoid him.

A second by-product of guilt is devaluation. We tend to not like or respect those who increase our guilt. The one who hurts the victim in shock experiments thinks less of him afterwards. It's the kind of rationalization that says the klutz deserved whatever he got. This is similar to what police discover in criminal investigations. After the crime, the guilty party sees the victim as having little worth. As ambassadors for Jesus Christ, our aim is to encourage people to love and worship our Lord. Making them feel guilty toward him produces the exact opposite result.

There is an ironic story about a boy who wouldn't eat his prunes at dinner. His mother made the ultimate threat. "God won't like it if you don't eat them," she declared. Yet he continued to sit stubbornly, so she sent him to his room. Later there was a severe thunderstorm. His mother tiptoed into the room to soothe him so he wouldn't be scared. But as it turned out he was sitting by the window watching the lightning play across the sky with an amused expression on his face. As she drew near, she overheard him say to himself, "Tch, tch! Such a fuss over a few lousy prunes." In this case the boy accepted his mother's judgment of guilt, but ended up viewing God as slightly ridiculous. Perhaps conviction of sin is best left to the Holy Spirit.

A third problem with guilt as a persuasive technique is that it usually gets positive results only in outward actions without a corresponding internal commitment. Although you might make Red Cross calls for Pete out of a sense of obligation, that kind of guilt wouldn't win you over to his cause. As stewards of the Great Commission, we've got to be concerned with more than outward compliance to the Christian faith.

Probably the most tragic side effect of loading guilt on another is that it can mess him up psychologically. The Christian therapist Paul Tournier writes:

For true guilt is precisely the failure to dare to be oneself. It is the fear of other people's judgment that prevents us from being ourselves, from showing our tastes, our desires, our convictions, from developing ourselves and from expanding freely according to our own nature. It is the fear of other people's judgment that makes us sterile, and prevents our bearing all the fruits that we are called to bear. "I was afraid," said the servant who hid his talent in the earth instead of putting it to use. (Matt. 25:25)[8]

I have a friend who was brought up in a Christian home where guilt was the main motivator. She was made to feel guilty about how little she prayed and read the Bible, about her use of time and money, about how little she witnessed to others—in fact, about anything concerning God. She's recently experienced a miraculous emo-

Drawing by Weber; © 1971 The New Yorker Magazine, Inc.

"Thunder and lightning is God's way of saying, 'How come you didn't eat your lima beans?' "

tional healing through the laying on of hands, and her faith in the Lord far outstrips mine. However, guilt leaves mental scars—she's unable to experience the joy and freedom in Christ which Paul speaks about in Galatians.

What then shall we conclude about the advisability of using guilt as a persuasive tool to bring men to God? Is guilt an effective motivator? At first blush the answer is yes. Guilt can produce immediate outward response to our urgings for Christian commitment. But in the long run, it also produces a devaluation of God, a desire to avoid him, and psychological scars which make it difficult to enjoy a relationship with him.

Does all this mean that men shouldn't feel guilty for turning their backs on God? By no means. True repentance comes from conviction of sin. But what I'm suggesting is that this kind of remorse isn't whipped up by the manipulations of man. It can come only from the Holy Spirit. Paul draws the distinction when he writes, "For godly grief produces a repentance that leads to salvation and brings no regret, but wordly grief produces death" (2 Corinthians 7:10).

The fruits of the Spirit are love, joy, peace, patience, kindness, goodness, faithfulness, gentleness, and self-control (Galatians 5:22, 23). These are not produced in others by making them feel guilty. They come through attraction to our Lord Jesus Christ. Abraham Lincoln had a folksy way of putting it: "You catch more flies with a teaspoon of honey than a bucket of spit."

6

Fear

Jonathan Edwards scared people. In his famous sermon, "Sinners in the Hands of an Angry God," Edwards pictured his eighteenth-century hearers as writhing spiders, dangling over the fiery pit of hell. God would contemptuously crush them under his feet so that their blood would splatter against the walls of the pit. To say that people felt fear is an understatement. Edwards literally scared them into heaven.

As Christians in the twentieth century, we may be embarrassed by the excesses of Edwards's scare tactics. I, for one, shy away from using such an extreme fear appeal. Yet at the same time I feel uneasy about completely throwing out fear as a way of motivating people to come to Jesus Christ. As the psalmist said, "The fear of the Lord is the beginning of wisdom" (Psalms 111:10) Our Lord himself seems to have occasionally sought a reaction of fear from his listeners. Jesus cursed the unproductive fig tree, warned people to stay awake in the parable of the foolish virgins, and foretold the doom of those who lead children astray. Any man who took his words seriously would feel at least a touch of terror.

At first blush, using fear as a means of persuasion seems rather straightforward. You merely present the possibility of a future occurrence that would be unpleasant to your listener. This could be an eternity in hell, lung cancer, an atomic explosion, a poor grade in school, a spanking, a divorce, drilling at the dentist's, rejection by friends—anything that your listener seeks to avoid. This creates an emotional reaction of fear which spurs the listener to adopt your way of avoiding that negative possibility—accept Jesus as Lord, stop smoking, advocate nuclear disarmament, study harder, stop fighting, seek marriage counseling, brush your teeth, use a deodorant, etc.

The results of this technique are often spectacular. When I was four years old, my parents spent a few months living in a house on Tampa Bay in Florida. The backyard ended abruptly at the edge of the Bay with an eight-foot drop-off down to the water. My mother portrayed all of the terrible things which could happen if I fell over the sea wall. I became convinced that as I hit the water I would simultaneously drown, dissolve in the polluted water, and be eaten by giant crabs. As a result, I not only stayed away from the edge, I never played in the backyard.

Fear appeals do not always get the desired results, however. They can backfire and actually drive the person in the opposite direction. When I was young, I showed a mild interest in airplanes. My parents tried to dissuade me from being a pilot by telling me of friends who had been killed in small plane crashes, horror stories of their own flights on commercial airlines, and of their disapproval if I was ever to become a pilot. My immediate reaction was to think that my parents were chicken, and I sought out every opportunity I could to ride in small airplanes. Whenever they talked about the dangers of flying, I would simply tune out. Today I am a pilot and flying is one of the great loves of my life.

It appears, therefore, that attempts to frighten others in order to persuade them have mixed results. Fear can be an effective motivator or it can boomerang and turn people off. In the rest of this chapter I'll present the results of research in persuasion and my own personal experience to indicate when fear appeals are helpful for the Christian advocate, and when they might hinder the cause of Christ.[9]

Suppose you are a participant in a research project to study the effects of fear on persuasion. You might experience something like this. Two weeks before the actual experiment, you fill out a questionnaire concerning your driving habits—what kind of car you drive, how many miles per year, accidents in the last three years, etc. Included in the form are questions concerning your attitudes toward seat belts and

"Ten...nine...eight...seven...six."

whether or not you actually wear them. When you arrive for the study, you are assigned to one of three communication groups. Each group sees a persuasive movie advocating the value of seat belts in saving lives plus an exhortation to use them.

The messages differ, however, in the amount of frightening material they contain. In the low fear group, you see statistics showing that your chance of surviving a crash is four times better with seat belts, or you listen to the National Safety Council's song, "Buckle Up for Safety." In the medium fear group, you watch in slow motion as a car containing wax dummies crashes into a brick wall at 30 mph. When seat belts aren't fastened, the dummies fly into the windshield and break apart. Or perhaps you see an interview with a policeman describing a crash victim who didn't wear a seat belt. In the high fear condition, you see films of actual crashes without seat belts—including blood spilling into the street, moans from the victims, and cries of anguish from relatives.

After the presentation you are asked to fill out a questionnaire concerning your attitude toward seat belts and your intention of wearing them in the future. If it was a well-designed project, someone would check a few weeks later to see if you were actually wearing the belts.

The purpose of this kind of study is to determine what level of threat is most effective. This type of research has been run with many kinds of people (old-young, educated-uneducated, extroverts-introverts, men-women) using various topics (auto safety, cancer, tooth decay, bomb shelters). Most studies show that *the moderate or medium fear appeal persuades people more than either the low or high scare attempts.* In other words, up to a certain point, the more fear you can get a person to feel, the more readily he will accept your solution. Once this point is exceeded, however, the more frightening the message, the more the person is scared off from your point of view.

The big question for the Christian witness is, of course, "How can I know when I've reached that point of optimum effectiveness?" Just what is a "moderate" amount of fear? How much fear is too much? The answer to these questions is not a simple one. To determine that maximum point of effectiveness, we must first determine why persuasion decreases with too much fear.

There are three possible explanations for the diminished success of high fear appeals. They can be summarized by the often heard comments of those who have been exposed to extremely threatening material.

"I was scared out of my mind."
"Aw, it'll never happen to me."
"I don't think it'll do any good."

"The old persuasive approach is out. From now on, they put out their campfires or you *bite* them."

These three reactions are examined below. Any one of the three is sufficient to explain why a highly frightening message often boomerangs on the persuader. An understanding of these explanations will help the Christian advocate to legitimately tap in to the honest fears of his audience without drawing a negative response.

"I WAS SCARED OUT OF MY MIND." We're all familiar with the physical feelings that go along with fear—heart pounding, butterflies in the stomach, throat dry, hands sweating, muscles tense. These things occur as the body is preparing itself for the supreme effort of either fight or flight. A certain amount of this aids persuasion. As the adrenalin is pumped throughout the body, a person becomes highly vigilant for a solution which will deliver him from the fearful situation. But emotional arousal can reach too high a pitch. A person can literally be "scared stiff." This is a state of panic in which the listener is no longer able to consider your solution. He is totally absorbed in his own fear.

This sort of fright feeds on itself. It's scary to be that afraid. (As Franklin Roosevelt said about the bank panic during the Depression, "The only thing we have to fear is fear itself.") Since it is so frightening, people seek to avoid the type of confrontation which produces high fear. They'll try to avoid the speaker and they won't pay attention. If they do hear him, they'll tend not to believe him, and they'll focus on how much they don't like him. (Note how similar these reactions are to the side effects of guilt presented in the previous chapter.)

The fact that high fear leads to avoidance can be seen in the reports that those who are most fearful of cancer are the ones who are least likely to see a doctor. As Christian communicators, we must be sensitive to the verbal and nonverbal signs of avoidance that will show our listener is too frightened to be able to intelligently respond to the gospel.

There are times when people can handle high fear and won't avoid a frightening message. The more experience we have with an issue or topic, the more we can realistically face threatening material. For example, a month after I began taking flying lessons, I started to read an article on heart attacks in the cockpit. I was terrified at the thought that I might keel over while flying. I put the magazine aside without knowing the author's recommendation. A few months ago I started reading a similar article. Although it was equally scary, I found myself considering each point carefully. As a result of my fear, I made an appointment for a full medical checkup.

Jonathan Edwards was able to take advantage of this phenomenon. His listeners had been concerned with the hereafter all of their lives. Heaven and hell were very real places that they frequently discussed. They were therefore unable to avoid the fearful implications of a life without Christ, whereas today's typical American listener— unsophisticated in theological truths—would be driven away by Edwards's hellfire and brimstone approach.

It's important for the Christian persuader to analyze his audience. The more experience and involvement a person has had with the matters of Jesus Christ, the more likely he is to respond to the threat of separation from God.

There is a second explanation for the fact that high fear appeals usually are not as effective as moderate appeals. It can be summed up in the statement:

"AW, IT'LL NEVER HAPPEN TO ME." Fear research has shown that it is difficult to predict how scared a person will actually be. Although the speaker may intend that his message be extremely frightening, it's quite possible that his audience will remain unshaken. The reason for this is that the amount of fear a person feels depends not only on how terrified he is of a future possibility, but also on his view of the probability of it happening *to him*. (Fear = Terror × Probability)

The idea of all my teeth falling out is terrifying—but I don't really think it's going to happen to me, so I experience little fear. The idea doesn't motivate me to brush my teeth. Since I eat lots of candy, however, I'm pretty sure the dentist is going to use his drill on me next month. It's only moderately painful, but since it's almost a sure thing, I feel real fear—enough to motivate me to brush three times a day.

Why are moderate fear appeals usually more persuasive than high ones? Because most extreme threats appear fairly remote. Subjectively, the more severe the threat, the less likely it seems to happen. The listener says to himself, "Aw, it'll never happen to me."

The implication of this phenomenon is that a high fear appeal can be a great motivating force—if a person believes it has a good chance of coming true. This is most likely when a similar catastrophe has hit close to home in the past. For example, my older brother died of pneumonia before I was born. My mother was naturally scared of me getting sick, so she dressed me in a snowsuit when the temperature dipped under 40°.

The persuader can simulate this "immediacy" by encouraging a person to role play the fearful experience. (See Chapter 7.) There's a smoking clinic near my home that uses this technique. They have a person pretend he's just found out that he has lung cancer and will die in three months. He talks to his doctor, his wife, his children, and his friends—all played by members of the clinic staff. This role play makes the actual possibility of cancer real to the patient—and the emotional impact of this fear induces him to stop smoking.

Perhaps the most effective fear appeal that I've used involves increasing the probability of a dreaded occurrence. Every summer I spend a week in Colorado with high school kids from my community who have little or no contact with the Christian faith. At the end of the week, I get together with those who have made a commitment to the Lord and read them Jesus' parable of the sower (Matthew 13:1-23). Here Jesus talks about four different soils or people. Three of the four are receptive to the gospel. I point out that this is similar to the percentage of kids at camp who have responded to the message of Christ during the week. In the parable, only one of the three soils produces a crop that lasts. I let the kids know that this is my experience from previous years—that only one out of three will be around the Christian faith a year later.

The high probability that he will abandon his faith is a very frightening idea to someone who has just trusted the Lord. I talk about the things they can do to insure their continued growth in Christ. I've had a number of kids tell me a year or two later, "That really scared me, Em. I decided right then and there that I was going to beat the odds." By increasing the probability of a feared outcome, we can increase the effectiveness of a fear appeal.

There's a third explanation for the fact that high fear appeals are usually ineffective. The person who is thoroughly convinced of an upcoming catastrophe often doubts the power of the solution to deliver him from it. He says in effect:

" I DON'T THINK IT'LL DO ANY GOOD." As I mentioned near the start of this chapter, persuasion through fear is a two-step process. First you present the threat, then a way of avoiding it. In order for the communication to be successful, the other person has to believe both parts of it—the fear appeal and the solution. High fear appeals often fail because the hearer just doesn't believe the solution is powerful enough to deliver him from extreme threat. "I don't think it'll do any good."

It's easier to scare someone than it is to take away his fear. The point at which fear appeals start to boomerang is when the fright outweighs the credibility of the solution. Think back to the experiment about seat belts. Somehow a narrow strip of cloth around his waist doesn't seem like a great solution to the person who has just seen all of the blood and guts of a fatal auto crash. We can see this problem in the field of political persuasion as well. A few years ago politicians of both parties used the phrase "law and order" to raise fears of being robbed or mugged in the street. The campaign was unsuccessful because the average voter didn't really believe that either party could do anything to reduce that threat. Let's face it, there just aren't that many "great solutions" floating around the world's great fears.

In order to avoid this problem of doubt, we need to make certain that the listener considers the solution at least as powerful as the threat. If we increase the level of fear, we must also increase the believability of the solution. The mouthwash industry has spent millions of dollars getting the American public to fear the possibility of bad breath. At least one company has now focused its advertising on the power of the product—Listerine. They stress how bad it tastes—and imply that anything so awful must kill a lot of germs.

This is similar to the experience of a medical supply firm which developed an effective antiseptic that didn't sting. The problem was that people wouldn't use it because they didn't believe it was strong enough to kill bacteria. When the company added alcohol to make it sting, sales rose sharply. (I've often noticed that non-Christians are suspicious of the too-easy solution of "believing in Christ." Perhaps by stressing the commitment involved in Christ's command to "take up your cross daily," we would make our message more credible.) It takes a highly believable solution to alleviate a high state of emotional tension. Research has shown that the best way to insure the believability of a solution is to have it presented by a highly credible source. (See Chapter 9, "Credibility.")

I might respond favorably to a high fear appeal involving gory car crashes if the National Safety Council or Ralph Nader said I would survive by wearing a shoulder harness. If I heard the same message from the company that was trying to sell the harness—forget it. Therefore the source of the message makes a big difference as to whether or not a fear appeal is successful.

The lesson for the Christian persuader is obvious. We are in the unique position of being able to offer the one great solution to the world's problems—Jesus Christ. Yet the world is unlikely to overcome its fear if we, the messengers, are not credible. The more we earn the respect and trust of another person, the more likely he is to see our Savior as the answer to his deepest fears.

I would also suggest that we make sure a person is likely to have confidence in our solution before we arouse his fears. The evangelist has traditionally presented man's sin with its consequent threat of hell first, and only then presented God's love as seen on the Cross. I find that it is better to first proclaim the person of Jesus Christ—his power, his wisdom, his love, his mercy, and his resurrection. This way the man knows he can have confidence in the Savior when his fears are later aroused.

* * * *

In the last few pages I've tried to show the limits on the use of fear as a persuasive device. Occasionally there are situations in which these limits can be exceeded and extreme fright is very effective. Acts 5 tells us that Ananias and Sapphira lied to the disciples about a contribution of land. When Peter confronts him with the truth, Ananias drops dead. Later Sapphira continues the deception, so Peter announces that she too will die. And she does!

Now let's consider the reasons for the persuasive impact of this fearful object lesson upon the church. These early Christians had already experienced God's power in many ways, and they had an abiding interest in matters common to the church. Therefore the threat did not cause the avoidance which would come from being scared out of their minds. The church was still small and localized. Many members actually witnessed the incident, and the rest soon heard about it. All of the Christians recognized that God knows the innermost secrets of the heart. It would be impossible for them to react to the incident by saying, "It could never happen to me." Nor could they doubt Peter's credibility. The Lord himself had placed Peter at the head of the church and had validated that leadership through many signs of power. If Peter said you could avoid a similar death by being honest about your gifts to the brethren, it was true.

This terrifying event was extremely persuasive. I doubt very much that anyone held out on the church again for a long time. "And great fear came upon the whole church, and upon all who heard of these things" (Acts 5:11). Most situations, however, don't lend themselves to the use of such high fear. A moderate or medium level of fear usually has a greater influence.

We can see, therefore, that there are three different guidelines to help us determine the point at which fear inhibits persuasion. When a threat appears so great that: 1) it causes mental panic, 2) seems unlikely to happen, or 3) has no believeable remedy, it ceases to be a positive influence. It's impossible to know for sure at exactly what point these reactions will occur. For the sake of both our listener and our message, it's wise to err on the side of too little fear than too much.

Some people maintain that fear is an illegitimate means of persuasion. I disagree. There are things in both this world and the next that *are* fearsome, and it's foolish to pretend that they don't exist. Fear can be a powerful motivator. As Christians, however, we need to use this persuasive technique carefully. We don't want to call men to Christ only to have them live in perpetual fear. "For God did not give us a spirit of timidity, but a spirit of power and love and self-control" (2 Timothy 1:7).

7

Role Play

Hunger has always been a stranger to me. My family was well off and we never failed to have plenty of food on the table. What's more, they were quality groceries. During the period of rationing in World War II, my parents traded gasoline stamps for food coupons so that we could have lots of fresh meat and vegetables. As an adult, I've continued to eat well. Because I'm blessed with a high metabolism rate, I've never had to diet or cut back on calories.

I'm quite aware that the majority of people around the world aren't as fortunate. I've seen pictures of starving children in Bangladesh, read statistics about famine in Haiti, and heard speakers describe the effects of malnutrition in rural Appalachia and urban ghettos. Despite this knowledge, the world hunger problem had always seemed rather remote to me. I'm not proud of this fact, but hunger occupied a low priority on my list of things to pray for and attempt to change.

Two years ago, however, Senator Mark Hatfield sponsored a Senate resolution calling for a National Day of Fasting and Prayer. A friend of mine suggested that I join him in a thirty-six hour fast in which we'd eat no food and drink only water. This was brand new to me. Despite the biblical injunction, I'd never fasted. I decided to give it a try and entered into a fast with eagerness and anticipation.

The first twelve hours I hardly noticed any difference. There was a slight desire for food, but nothing special. I was definitely hungry the second twelve hours, but I also experienced an unusual clarity of thought and ability to concentrate in prayer. This feeling fled as I began the second day of the fast. I was ravenously hungry. All I could think of was food. We had a communion service near the end of the thirty-six hours. Although my portion of bread was only a small cube, I eagerly waited for it to be served. As I placed it in my mouth, I didn't remember the Lord or his death for us—all I thought of was the taste of it and that I wished there was more.

It was at this point that hunger became a reality to me. Of course the hunger I experienced was ridiculously minor. Thirty-six hours without food for a well-fed adult is nothing comparable to the chronic gnawing pain felt by a child existing on 800 calories a day. But as fleeting as the feeling was, it caused me to reorder my whole attitude toward food and those who don't have enough of it. Since that time I've started praying in earnest, joined with other Christians in the organization Bread for the World, contributed an increased amount of money for famine relief, and contacted my congressman about various hunger-related legislation.

In short, I've become persuaded. But this is a special kind of persuasion—a self-persuasion. It came about because for a few moments I ceased to be Em Griffin and imagined what it was to be someone who would be hungry forever. I crawled around in another skin and saw life through different eyes. This experience overcame my natural resistance to get involved in the plight of others. The process that persuaded me is called role play, and it's a fantastically powerful way to get people to consider new ideas. In fact, role play is the most persuasive means I know of to melt others toward a different position. In the rest of the chapter, we'll look at the technique of role play—what it is, why it works, and how to encourage others to do it.

ROLE PLAY VS. ROLE TENDING. We're all familiar with kids pretending to be their parents. The boy dons a hat and picks up a briefcase—"I'm Daddy going to work." His sister goes to the stove, flips an imaginary pancake, and calls the children for breakfast. "That's how Mommy does it," she says. This isn't just idle make-believe. An important process of self-persuasion is taking place. As children role

Drawing by Lorenz; © 1970 The New Yorker Magazine, Inc.

play their parents they identify with them, see the world through their eyes, and ultimately adopt most of their attitudes. This pretending is a necessary process if kids are to grasp their parents' values. As one communication specialist puts it, without identification there is no persuasion.

Role play is a means of getting a person to identify with someone else. There's an old Indian saying—"You can't understand a man until you walk a mile in his moccasins." Role play is a technique that says, "OK, put them on." For a few moments you're no longer yourself—you're him. How do those shoes feel? What's it like being him?

There's all forms of active role play. I can pretend to be an actual person like my father or boss, or I can imagine that I'm a hypothetical person who holds attitudes different from mine. I might use props and costuming to stimulate my imagination, but it's also possible to mentally create the setting without these aids. There may be other people involved in the drama, or it could be a one-man show. But whatever the form of the role play, there's a tacit agreement between the actor and everyone present that for a few moments, he'll cease to be himself and will rather adopt the world view of the character he's playing.

If all this sounds a bit strange to you, it's because we don't do much of this kind of thing in the adult world. Children appear to try on different roles spontaneously, but somehow it seems undignified to grown-ups. As a matter of fact, I'm hard-pressed to think of any adult setting—apart from dramatic theatre and group therapy—where overt role play is a regular feature. But if active role play is a stranger to most people, there's a more passive form that is common to many. Let's call this "role tending."

By role tending I refer to a purely mental activity. The drama goes on in the mind rather than being physically enacted. Actors are involved in role play. An audience which empathizes with the characters being portrayed is role tending. We often role tend when we read a good novel, see a well done movie or TV show, or, of course, when we attend a live play. We watch someone else in his role and imagine ourselves going through the same thing. This happens in real life too. Anytime we rejoice with those who rejoice, weep with those who weep, laugh with those who laugh, etc., we are mentally taking the role of the other and identifying with him.

Role play requires physical movement and verbal expression. Role tending is a more passive armchair activity. Both are strong persuasive tools. Anytime we can induce another person to temporarily "try on" a new belief, we stand a good chance of influencing him in that direction. I'll illustrate that fact from a role play experiment designed to help people stop smoking.[10]

LET'S PRETEND. It's quite difficult to persuade people to stop smoking. There are a number of reasons for this. Tobacco is an addictive drug. Remove it and the system cries out for its return. In addition, the smoker has psychological needs which are met by cigarettes. Take them away and he hurts. And then a high-powered advertising industry has worked hard to equate smoking with love, glamour, maturity, relaxation, and almost anything else you might desire. Finally, the smoker builds up all sorts of mental rationalizations as to why cigarettes aren't really that bad for him.

Since smoking is a practice highly resistant to change, it provides a good test for the effectiveness of role play as a persuasive technique. Two Yale researchers went to a girls' school and interviewed a large number of coeds who were regular smokers. Some smoked as little as four or five cigarettes a day, while others were veritable volcanos, spewing the ashes produced by three packs from morning to night. The girls averaged a daily consumption of twenty-four cigarettes—just over a pack a day. The professors assigned each gal to one of three activities or conditions—role play, role tending, or no activity. There were the same number of girls in each condition, and the average of each group was twenty-four smokes a day.

When I was growing up, one cigarette company advertised: "We're tobacco men, not medicine men. For a treat instead of a treatment, try Old Gold." The girls in the role play condition weren't in for a treat—they got the treatment instead. One of the experimenters met with each gal individually. He told her that they wanted to test her acting ability—her capacity to improvise and throw herself into a scene. She was to pretend to be a patient who had sought out a doctor's help because of a continual cough. She'd come in a couple of days ago for a series of tests and was now returning to get the results. There was no script. She could respond to the other actor in whatever way she desired. The researcher then ushered her into a room that was decked out like a doctor's office. There was a scale, sterilizer, thermometer, fluorescent light for reading X rays, and a medical school diploma on the wall. The room even smelled of disinfectant. The second experimenter was dressed like a physician—white lab coat and a stethoscope around his neck—and he spoke in an authoritative professional tone.

He came right to the point. The chest X rays gave a positive indication of lung cancer. This diagnosis had been confirmed by the chemical lab tests. There was no question but that this condition had been developing for a long time. The "doctor" then paused to let the girl respond. Often she would start talking about how she knew she'd been smoking too much. Eventually most asked what could be done.

The doctor was not optimistic. "We need to operate immediately.

Can you be prepared to check into the hospital tomorrow afternoon? There's about an even chance we can catch the malignancy, but of course the opposite possibility must be faced.'' At this point the play could go in a number of directions. The girls might express fear for her life, anguish over broken plans for graduation, hesitancy over how to tell her parents or fiancé, anger at God for this cruel blow, or disbelief that it was really happening to her. In this last case the doctor would assure her that she was free to consult another physician, but that there was no question that the tissue was cancerous. No matter what direction the role play took, the patient got caught up in the situation and became emotionally involved with the link between smoking and cancer.

The girls in the role tending condition didn't get to be in the play. They got to hear the dialogue on tape. The room was equipped with a hidden microphone, so that the role tending smokers could hear the mini-drama without affecting what happened.

The girls in the no treatment condition neither heard nor participated in the role play, yet they served a valuable purpose. The basis of any persuasion experiment is comparison, and the researchers needed a control group against which to base the effectiveness of role play and role tending treatments.

The professors waited two weeks for the effects of the role play to take hold and then surveyed the cigarette consumption of each girl. Not surprisingly, the no treatment subjects were still puffing away at a rate of twenty-four/day. Those who heard the role play cut their habit to an average of eighteen/day—a drop of 25 percent. And the coeds who had actually participated in the emotional drama were down to fourteen/day—a significant reduction of well over one-third.

When I present this study to my college students, a few scoff at the results. They say it's not such a big deal since no one actually quit smoking. They forget that fourteen/day is just an average. Some girls were unaffected, others cut back, and some quit "cold turkey." They also fail to appreciate what a wrenching thing it is for the habitual smoker to cut down. Other students raise a much more pertinent question: Did the effects of role play and role tending last over time? It's one thing to stimulate short-term withdrawal and quite another to effect a permanent change.

After eight months there had been some slippage. The role play subjects went up slightly to an average of fifteen/day. The role tending group had a similar rise to nineteen/day. Despite this slight regression, there was still a marked difference between those in the role play and role tending conditions and those who received no treatment. The Yale profs concluded that their experiment was a success.

Then there was an interesting development. About a month later, the government released the Surgeon General's report linking smoking with cancer. This announcement hit the nation like a bomb. In unequivocal terms it said that smoking is harmful to your health. The report was released on a Saturday so that it wouldn't kick off a stock market crash. As it was, cigarette sales plummeted throughout the country.

The two role play researchers began to wonder what effect all this was having on their experimental subjects. They decided to take another measure a month after the Surgeon General's report came out. They found that like everyone else, the no treatment girls drastically cut their smoking. They were down to eighteen/day. Would this drop be paralleled by role play treatment subjects who had already cut their consumption ten months before? The answer was yes. Those who'd heard the role play dropped to thirteen/day and those who had acted were down to ten/day. Both of these levels were well below the initial experimental results.

As everyone now knows, the effects of the U.S. Government report were short-lived. Within a few months cigarette sales snapped back to normal. Good intentions gave way to habits built up over a lifetime. Many folks who'd always claimed that they could take it or leave it found that tobacco was something they could only take. This fact was mirrored in the behavior of the no treatment college coeds. A survey taken nine months after the Surgeon General's announcement showed that they were almost back where they started—twenty-three/day. But lo and behold—the same survey revealed that the girls involved in the role play treatment substantially maintained their new low level. Role tending subjects averaged fifteen/day and role play participants averaged twelve/day.

In case you've found all these cigarettes per day figures confusing, I've tried to sort them out in the following graph. Note that the twelve/day rate with which the role play girls concluded is exactly half of where they started, and it's also half the amount with which the control group ended. Note also that this low cigarette use was maintained a full year and a half after the simple role play procedure. Obviously, "Let's pretend..." is a very powerful way to introduce attitude and behavior change.

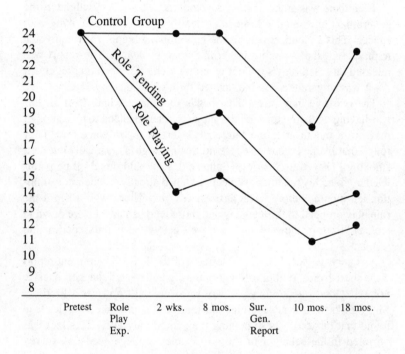

It's not enough, however, to know that role play is a powerful persuasive technique. As Christians desiring to influence others for the cause of Christ, we must grasp *why* role play is so successful. Only in this way will we be able to structure exercises which will encourage people to fulfill his two great commandments—loving God and loving man. In the rest of the chapter I'll present the different forces involved in role play's effectiveness. The personal examples I'll use will each illustrate a particular dynamic and will also suggest various ways of encouraging others to try it.

Courtesy PARADE magazine.

"Pretend you're somebody else and gossip about you."

ACTIVE PARTICIPATION. Let's face it—most persuasion attempts bore us to tears. We gaze idly at the TV set and can't remember the name of the product touted in the last commercial. We sit passively in a church pew glancing every two minutes at our watch to figure out when the sermon will be over. Lunch with the insurance man would be intolerable if it wasn't for the lunch. These attempts at influence are one-way efforts. The salesman talks, the customer listens. It's quite possible to just sit there and not deal with what's being said. The only energy required is to sign on the dotted line.

Role play, on the other hand, demands involvement. It's emotional. It stirs up the juices. The cognitive effort required to portray another person's attitude guarantees a high level of attention. The role player doesn't have the option of turning out unwanted ideas—he must actively grapple with them.

This happened to me when I role played my father. I never knew my dad well. When I was growing up, he worked long hours at a metropolitan newspaper. It seemed to me he was never home. As have other grown sons, I often wondered how dad really felt about me. Was he proud of me? Had I hurt him? Did he love me? I never had a chance to really find out because he died shortly after I finished college. My mother gave assurances of his great love for me. A friend told how often he boasted about my accomplishments. A psychologist pointed out that his behavior revealed how important I was to him. I listened but did not hear. I was immune to their attempts to persuade me. My father remained an aloof and detached figure.

Then a few years ago, I took part in a small group seminar on experimental methods for teachers. In one of the exercises, we divided into pairs. I was with a fellow about my age named Bill Howlett. The leader instructed us to role play our same sex parent. I was supposed to be Mr. Griffin, Em's father, and Bill was to become Mr. Howlett, Sr. We were to talk about our sons with each other—describing them, telling what we liked, sharing those things about them that disturbed us. In short, I was to try to see myself through my dad's eyes.

It was a totally absorbing experience. Although I was rather hesitant at the start due to my uncertainty of how my dad really *did* view me, I quickly warmed to the task. I recalled the fun times we'd had together. I told of my dreams for Em's future, and my disappointments when I couldn't spend more time with him. With a sad sigh, I related how Em didn't seem to want much to do with me by the time he got to high school. About five minutes into the exercise, I looked Mr. Howlett square in the eyes and stated with conviction, "I'm not sure he ever knew—but I loved him." Suddenly it dawned on me that it was really so. With tears in my eyes I broke from the role and blurted out to my partner, "It's true! He actually did love me. I just never felt it before."

Role tending does not automatically require the same expenditure of energy inherent in role play. Perhaps this is one of the reasons why the actor is usually more affected by his performance than is the audience. But it's quite possible for the role tender to get caught up in the human drama before his eyes. There are millions of people who expend enormous cognitive resources following every twist of their favorite TV soap opera during the day or the latest move of Kojak or Rhoda at night. This vicarious emotional response happened to Bill Howlett during our parental role play. He told me later that he was gripped by a new appreciation of his own dad's care and concern as he listened to my recital. It obviously occurred in the smoking experiment where role tenders were persuaded almost as much as the players themselves.

So active participation is one explanation for role play's effectiveness. The implications for the Christian persuader are clear— monologue is out; dialogue is in.

FANTASY. The imagination is a powerful persuader. Once I start to daydream about surging down a country road on a motorcycle, it's only a short step to buying a Kawasaki to "let the good times roll." We tend to act on the basis of the pictures in our mind.

Some people have vivid imaginations. Mention that smoking causes cancer and they immediately call up a picture of a hollow-chested smoker coughing consumptively as he's being wheeled into the operating room. Role play won't increase their susceptibility to influence because they automatically visualize the consequences of an action. But others among us are a bit more dull. We need help before we can picture what effect an idea will have on our lives. Role play is one such aid. It's an artificial technique which helps us to fantasize the future.

Weight watching clinics use role play to motivate their clients to reduce. The overweight person knows too well what it's like to be fat, but he has a tough time picturing himself being slim. Therefore the staff has him act out a scene in which he pretends to buy clothes when he is three sizes smaller than his present girth. This lets him test the benefits of being thin. They use another role play device which helps the patient anticipate the actual feeling of weighing less. For one week the client is required to wear a ten-pound weight belt. He's instructed to remove it a day or two before he returns to the clinic. The contrast is amazing. He's much less tired when he goes through the day without carrying the excess weight. The clinic staff merely point out the obvious—think how much better you'll feel when you take off another ten pounds. It works!

The power of fantasy to change attitudes and behavior can be seen in the movie *Jaws*. The film graphically shows a killer shark attacking swimmers at a New England coastal resort. This is fiction—make-believe. But the images become so deeply stenciled in the brain that applications for lifeguard positions fell off 50 percent along the Atlantic seaboard the year the movie came out. Once you've had those pictures projected on the brain pan, you simply can't say, "It'll never happen to me." Personally, I'm a strong swimmer and have never been concerned about sharks. After seeing *Jaws* I'm quite happy that my swimming is done in Lake Michigan.

Jesus used drama to give his words greater impact. He said:

"I am the vine" and made the best wine.
"I am the bread of life" and multiplied the loaves.
"I am the light of the world" and gave sight to the blind man.
"I am the resurrection and the life" and raised Lazarus.

We could do worse than to follow his example in our attempts to extend his kingdom. The play *Godspell* had a profound effect on me. The loving way it showed Jesus saying good-bye to his disciples before his capture brought forth tears of gratefulness. Equally powerful was the portrayal of Thomas Moore in *A Man for All Seasons*. His courage to die to preserve the truth did more to strengthen my commitment to righteousness than any ten sermons I've heard on not conforming to the world. Imagery is a potent, persuasive tool.

THE PERFECT ARGUMENT. I'm constantly amazed at the many different ways God draws men to himself. Recently I was in a sharing group of ten people where we went around and told why we were part of the Christian faith. Nine distinct reasons were offered. One man became a Christian because he was convinced that the resurrection was real. Another was scared into the fellowship by the threat of hell. A middle-aged woman allowed that she had entered the faith because it was important to her parents, whereas a teenager said he wanted more purpose in life than his folks had been able to offer. Personally, I was looking for friendship.

Can you picture trying to create one persuasive message which would have convinced all these people to turn to Christ? It boggles the imagination. The very thing that would appeal to one person would turn the next off. Different folks require different strokes. In addition, you might not even think of the argument that would prove compelling to a third person.

But role play can overcome this obstacle. In role play, a person comes up with his own reasons for change. Since he knows what's going on in his head better than anyone else, he's in the best position to come up with something that's impressive. In other words, his arguments are tailor-made to hit the points where he's most vulnerable to influence. Like the final piece of a jigsaw puzzle, the material he puts into his act is exactly shaped to fit his mental map. Thus role play is really a process of self-persuasion.

I saw this happen when our suburban neighborhood found out that a black family was moving into a home on our block. I wish I could report that all the people were ready to meet the new homeowners with open arms, but it wasn't so. One lady was particularly vocal in her opinion that property values would fall. She couldn't understand why these people didn't want to "stick with their own kind." Repeatedly she'd end her tirade with, "Why do they want to come here, anyway?"

I tried to answer her question. I pointed out that this family had a right to live as much as we did, that they were probably looking for better schools, that he was a research chemist in a nearby hospital and wanted to be near his work, and about ten other reasons as well. All this fell on deaf ears. My wife, who hasn't a persuasive bone in her body, was much smarter than I. When our neighbor asked her the "Why do they . . ." question, Jeanie bounced it right back to her. "I don't know, Marion. Why do *you* think they want to move here? Why go through such a hassle?"

At first the woman claimed there was no good reason—that it didn't make sense. But when Jeanie persisted, she began to struggle to answer her own question. "Well, they probably want to get away from Chicago. The city's such an impersonal and unfriendly place to live. I know if I were them I'd want to get away from all those gangs. I'd want to come to a place like this where people are warm."

The impartial reader may pick up a certain amount of irony in her statement, but note what's happening. Jeanie's response induced the neighbor to role play the black family's situation. She began to generate reasons that would justify the people's desire to move. The reasons she came up with weren't particularly convincing to me. In fact I'm not sure that the city is cold and unfriendly, but that's neither here nor there. They were *her* reasons and they convinced *her*. Although she didn't cease to be a bigot overnight, she at least stopped her public resistance to the family's entry onto our block. She even decided to bake some cookies for the new folks so they'd know it was a friendly neighborhood—not like Chicago.

Role play is most effective when the actor is free to improvise—to interject his own ideas. If he's tied to a script, he'll merely mouth someone else's thoughts, and these may not meet his objections. But if he has to create his own material in support of a previously unacceptable position, he'll usually come up with the perfect argument—the one that convinces him.

JUST PLAIN FUN. So far I've suggested three possible reasons for role play's effectiveness in melting people's resistance—it compels active participation, it stimulates fantasy, and it generates the best possible argument for changing opinion. There's a fourth possibility that sounds simplistic but shouldn't be overlooked. Role play is fun.

Most of us possess a touch of ham. With a little encouragement we'll toss ourselves into a game of charades, a skit, or a full-scale production. What's more, we'll enjoy it. There's an inward satisfaction which comes from stepping outside ourselves and successfully pretending to be someone else. The pleasure is doubled if there's an appreciative audience. All of this good feeling can positively affect the actor's attitude toward the position he proclaims. It's as if the enjoyment of the performance spills over into the content and makes it more acceptable. This happened to me when I was in college.

It took place in a speech class where I was paired with a fellow to debate another team. The issue was wiretapping. We were assigned to attack the legality and morality of electronic eavesdropping. In this post-Watergate era that would be a simple task, but at the time most people were caught up with the possibility that these technological discoveries might offer ways of preventing crime. Up until the debate I was mildly in favor of wiretapping.

The day for the debate came and my partner didn't show up. It was two against one. Both students of the affirmative side made strong cases and I had to refute them not only with my planned speech, but with an impromptu rebuttal as well. After it was all over, I mentally gave myself a pat on the back. This internal reward reflected the satisfaction I felt at covering for my absent partner. I also received an external reward from the class which voted my side the winner. As I look back, it was one of my most enjoyable days in college. Not surprisingly, I've been strongly opposed to wiretapping ever since.

So often attempts at persuasion are either dreary on the one hand, or obnoxious on the other. This is one of the real advantages of role play. It can be fun.

SAVING FACE. There's an area of persuasion research that's called "counter attitudinal advocacy." This is merely a specialized form of role play. It consists of asking a person to write an essay or deliver a speech advocating a position which runs counter to his present attitude—hence the name, counter attitudinal advocacy. People who agree to do this usually end up shifting their opinion. Why? The answer runs something like this.

If I freely profess an opinion to others that I don't hold privately, I find myself in a bind. There'd be no problem if I'd been coerced into my statement. In that case I would have said what I said because I had to. But if my statement was voluntary, I've trapped myself in a glaring inconsistency. I like to think of myself as reasonable, so something's got to give. If I take back what I've said, I'll look like a wishy-washy fool. So I go the other route and rationalize. "Why am I saying this? I'm not the kind of person to say one thing and believe another. I guess I really do believe it." I justify my public statement by changing my mind.

I've seen high school kids talk themselves into considering the Christian faith through this exact process. In a group meeting I'll suggest they list all of the possible benefits that they've heard or that they can think of for being a Christian. I stress that they don't have to actually believe that these things will really come to one who follows Christ, just that they might. I'll then open the meeting up to anyone who wants to throw in an idea. They're completely free to participate or remain silent. Most of these kids aren't Christians, yet they come up with dozens of great reasons why they should trust God—and they do so in the company of others. I find that they usually remember best what they said themselves. Often they come to believe it and act upon it.

* * * *

By now you can probably tell I'm sold on the use of role play for a Christian purpose. I'll have people pretend to be Peter when he meets Christ on the beach after the resurrection, a few days after he denied him. What will Jesus say to him now? What would he say to us? I'll have Sunday school teachers take the role of their students so they can discover which lessons will go and which ones will bomb. In family groups I'll have parents play their children and kids act out their parents. In order that they might "have the mind of Christ" as Paul charges, I'll have believers try to imagine that they are God and write a personalized letter to themselves from him.

Of course I'm not alone in urging the Christian's use of role play to foster change. The traditional Bible story format of Christian education encourages role tending. The Serendipity series of workbooks goes one step further by placing the reader in the biblical event and then asking what response he would make in that situation. There are role play games like Urban Dynamics which stimulate a social awareness of the plight of the poor. Perhaps the best use of role play that I've heard is put out by the Mennonite church in their series of radio spots entitled "Choice."

The target audience of "Choice" is the businessman returning from work to his suburban home. Each five-minute segment is aired on a secular station during the commuter rush hour. As he drives along, the man has little problem picturing himself in the dramatic situation. Each story is concerned with business deals, family problems, weekend recreation, or sexual relationships. It's where he's at. The programs are not miniature morality plays with a tag end sermon. Each spot presents one ethical dilemma that he might well have to face in the future, if he hasn't encountered it already. The series raises the questions of what God would have him do and presents a series of alternatives. No right answer is given.

"Choice" calls for active participation. At the end of each program, the narrator asks what they would do in the situation and reminds them that it's their choice. He gives an address so the listener can send for a booklet offering help in ethical decisions. I'm sure the pamphlet is persuasively written, but I doubt that it can match the impact of self-persuasion fostered by the "Choice" role play.

Most people who pick up this book desire to be change agents—people used by God to stimulate Christian evangelism and growth. As you've been reading this chapter, chances are that you've thought about some situation of possible influence. What do you want to accomplish? Is there a way that role play could achieve that better than a straight persuasive message? Call to mind the faces of the people you want to influence. What's the best way to encourage them to enter into a role play drama? Don't dismiss the idea too quickly. Be creative. In the words of the Alka-Seltzer role play, "Try it, you'll like it!"

MOLD

Incentives

You just never know where you'll discover persuasive excellence. A few years back I heard of a foreman on the San Francisco docks whose work record was nothing short of phenomenal. His gang of stevedores off-loaded twice as much cargo with only one-third the breakage of any other crew. Needless to say, the shippers were eager to discover the secret of his success. They found that it lay in his ability to get the men to use the hand dollies to move cases rather than muscling them by hand. This was no mean feat. Apparently the longshoremen thought it sissy to use the one-man hand carts, preferring to show their manliness by lifting and carrying the cases themselves. Even the name "dolly" argued against their use.

So how did he do it? It wasn't his pleasing personality. By any standard the guy was surly, crude, and vulgar. Some checking revealed, however, that he always gave advice in terms of how it would benefit the other worker. "Save your back, stupid, use the dolly." Other foremen would yell that the rules required them to use the hand carts or they'd plead for them to be more careful. But our man seemed to understand intuitively that people are motivated by how they'll stand to gain or lose in the process.

The "minimax" states this systematically. The minimax isn't a new

dress style or pocket calculator. Rather it's a principle of human behavior that answers the question, "Why do we do what we do?" It
answers that *humans act so as to maximize their benefits and minimize
their costs*. The minimax suggests that our brains act as a calculator—
continually computing the outcome of possible actions on the basis of
rewards minus losses. The behavior that has the highest payoff is what
we do.

"Wait a minute," you say. "That sounds awfully selfish. That kind of
'what's in it for me' attitude may be OK for the average Joe, but I'm a
Christian and God calls me to love my neighbor, walk an extra mile,
and turn the other cheek. Are you saying that I always act to increase
my benefits?" Sure. I do too. When we become Christians, we don't
check out on the human race. But hopefully God has begun his work in
us and we're starting to have the mind of Christ. This means that we're
slowly changing our opinion as to what makes for a positive outcome.
It's just that as Christians, we've decided to play our lives to God.
We've come to consider his smiling "Well done, my good and faithful
servant" a tremendous benefit, whereas many non-Christians couldn't
care less. Yes, we do the same benefit-cost figuring as everyone else.

God doesn't seem to be particularly bothered by the fact that we
determine our actions by totaling up rewards and costs. The writer of
Hebrews states that the hope of divine reward is a condition of genuine
faith. "For whoever would draw near to God must believe that he exists
and that he rewards those who seek him" (Hebrews 11:6.) Jesus himself advocated considering the cost of following him before becoming a
disciple (Luke 14:28). In fact, we might take a look at his famous
"Come unto me . . ." offer in the light of the minimax:

Action: Take my yoke upon you
High Benefit: Rest for those who are weary and heavy laden
Low Cost: Easy yoke, light burden

(See Matthew 11:29, 30.)

All of this suggests that we'll be way ahead of the game if we learn to
make our persuasive appeal in terms of what it will do for the other
person. Business and industry has picked up on this idea in their advertising. One tool company switched from talking about their electric drill

to describing what the tool would do for the buyer. They said simply, "We sell holes." This makes so much sense that it's hard to believe that we in the church ignore the fact that benefits are what people are waiting to hear. But we often do. We tell them what they should believe or what they ought to do without making any effort to show the advantages that come from God's way. All of us need incentives before we change. Incentive research has discovered that some ways of offering rewards and punishments are more influential than others. In the next few pages I'll offer some specific advice based on these findings.

MORE CARROTS, FEWER STICKS. For centuries the debate has raged. Which motivates better, the carrot or the stick—reward or punishment? My own limited experience in a donkey basketball game produced mixed results. The donkey ate my carrots and absorbed my whacks with equal unconcern. The only thing which seemed to really interest him was pitching me off his back. But if the answer is cloudy concerning dumb beasts, it comes through crystal clear in the case of human beings. We respond much better to praise than we do to criticism, rewards more than punishment, and positive reinforcement over negative incentives.

This is one of those things that's so easy to accept in theory, but so hard to put into practice. A colleague of mine points out the problem we have giving positive feedback. If our child shows us a school paper and he's spelled yellow Y E L L A W, we automatically tell him that the A is wrong. He suggests that we might try the positive approach instead. Something like, "That's great, Johnny. The Y, the E, both L's and the W are all correct!" Of course this strikes us as ludicrous, probably because giving constant approval for little things is so foreign to the way we normally respond. Perhaps that reticence to affirm others has something to do with our low batting average in influencing others.

I had a brief fling as a hockey coach where I decided to use only positive feedback to get the boys to play a better game. The loss of our first seven games dictated that I experiment around. I purchased a batch of red stickers about the size of a penny. I told the boys that these were merit awards to place on their helmets and that they'd get them at the end of each game for outstanding play. Of course they received a sticker if they scored, but they also got them for good passes, hard checks,

hustling, and enthusiasm. Sometimes it was hard to pick out anything praiseworthy. I finally told one guy I'd give him a sticker if he was able to take one turn on the ice without falling down. When he did it, he was as proud as if he'd just scored the winning goal. Another player had the bad habit of taking shots at our own net. (Can you see why we were 0—7?) We made a deal that he'd get a sticker if our goalie didn't have to make a save on any of his errant passes. It took an extraordinary amount of willpower not to criticize when a boy did something stupid or dumb, but by biting my tongue and gritting my teeth I was able to keep silent. I even discovered that these ten-year-olds usually knew when they were doing something wrong anyway. They didn't need me to confirm it.

The stickers were presented publicly in the locker room amid much praise and team applause. They came to have a tremendous value to the kids. One mother called me before a game saying that her son had pneumonia, but still wanted to come that night so he could have a shot at earning a sticker. Would I please talk to him and tell him he could go double or nothing when he was healthy?

Did all this do any good? Yes. We continued to lose the next two weeks, but began to play better. We tied the next game and won the final four. We even got to the championship game in the playoffs. What's more significant, they had a good time. Whereas most teams broke up at the end of the season, our guys all decided that they'd like to stay together for the next go-round.

Some people object to using a preponderance of positive rewards on

Drawing by W. Miller; © 1969 The New Yorker Magazine, Inc.

the grounds that the other person might get spoiled. They're afraid that compliments and praise might go to his head and give him a puffed up idea of his own ability or importance. I don't share this fear. The world is a pretty cruel place, and the average guy is going to get lots of mean jabs and harsh knocks as he works his way through life. If we can give some honest affirmation to counterbalance the self-doubts he'll naturally feel, let's do it. "Love is kind." It's also persuasive. If you honestly care about the other person and desire to show him a better way—try the carrot.

SHAPING. The process of using incentives to change the way another person acts goes under many names. Traditionally it's been called *shaping*. More recently the term *behavior modification*, or just B-mod, has come into vogue. From my candle-making analogy, I see it as molding. All of these labels suggest that we can't change someone's pattern of behavior instantaneously, it takes time. Each use of a reward or punishment has only a slight effect on another's actions. But a series of small changes can total up to a whopping difference over time. Let me illustrate.

Suppose you were given the job of training a pigeon to walk in a perfect figure eight.[11] You might easily despair of ever accomplishing the task, for pigeons aren't known for either their intelligence or desire to do what man wants. Certainly you'd be frustrated if you tried to "persuade" the bird all at once. But the job could be done. All it would take is some patience on your part, a good supply of corn, and a hungry pigeon.

I'd suggest starting by rewarding the bird whenever he walks around. There's no way he's going to do a figure eight while he's resting. Don't worry about how fast he goes, or in what direction. Just give him a kernel of corn when he moves. I guarantee that you'll very quickly have a moving pigeon. Once he's ambulatory, you can begin to work on getting him to follow a circular path. If he goes straight or veers to the right, withhold the food. You can even give him an uncomfortable tap on the head to stimulate him to try something else. When he turns left though, offer him some more food. If you're consistent with your rewards you'll soon have a bird that goes around in circles—to the left. But that's not what you want him to do. After he goes one complete revolution to the left, you want him to turn to the right and do another circle to complete the figure eight. This is tough. You've instilled the idea of going only to the left and that's hard to modify. But sometime—just through random movement—the pigeon is going to circle to the left and then break right. That's the time to reward him, at that instant. It'll take awhile, but the bird will catch on that he only gets a kernel of corn if he does one circle to the left and then one circle of the same size to the right on top of that. When the whole process is complete, you'll have a figure eight that's worthy of an Olympic figure skater.

I must confess that I feel somewhat uneasy as I read back over what I've just written. It sounds so manipulative. I have no qualms about selectively reinforcing a pigeon if it serves a good purpose. But how about fellow human beings? Doesn't a systematic plan of behavior modification run counter to the ethic of increasing responsible choice? Not necessarily. It depends on whether the person whose actions are being affected is aware of what's going on, and also on whether he likes it. If the process is a covert attempt to change another without him being aware that he's being influenced, then I think it does have a sinister ring. But if he understands that you're trying to help him change his actions, and he's willing to change, then it's OK. I can think of a number of examples, but perhaps one from my family will suffice.

I want Jim to cut our grass, and to do it in a way that leaves the lawn looking good, the lawnmower in decent condition, and his body in one piece. Two years ago this goal seemed unattainable. When he first took on the yard, it was a moot point as to which came out of the encounter looking worse. The grass was cut in wildly uneven rows, the blade of the power mower was nicked by rocks, and Jim had barely avoided amputating his foot. He assured me that he had nothing against cutting the lawn per se, it was just that it was hard work and he'd rather be doing something else. I decided it was time to shape behavior through incentives.

Because I love my son, I focused on the safety aspects first. I paid him a dollar for one hour of work by the clock, and didn't worry about how much got done. We concentrated on how to start the mower, shutting the motor off when adjusting the blade height, and never lifting up on the handle when turning at the end of a row. I was free with praise and worked with him the whole hour. These were both pluses to him. After safe habits had become second nature, I started to reinforce actions that made the lawn look good—overlapping rows, keeping the clippings out of the flower bed, changing blade height when mowing over a hill. I now adjusted the pay according to how well the job was done. I also fixed him a Coke over ice halfway through when the quality looked good. By now I no longer had to work with him, just check in the middle and at the end of the job. When quality work became a habit, I switched to quantity as the focus of my rewards. Jim wanted new goalie pads for hockey. We agreed that I'd buy them if he would take care of the lawn for the rest of the summer and fall. This meant he could take as long or as short as he wanted to finish the lawn each week. Because there was no advantage to stretching it out, he whipped through the task in about half the time it had taken him before.

Now was there anything underhanded or manipulative about our arrangement? I don't think so. He clearly understood that I was aiming to change him into a first-rate grass cutter. Although he wasn't wildly excited about this goal, neither did he have any moral objection. I wasn't trying to get him to do something that would violate his personality. By using a mixed bag of benefits, I took my son's rather gross and random behavior and shaped it into a narrow pattern of effectiveness. He was free to decide at any time that the goodies I offered weren't worth it, and I was equally free to choose a different method of getting the lawn cut. I ended up with a well cared-for yard. He ended up with some dollars, words of praise, a feeling of accomplishment, and a set of goalie pads. Not a bad trade all around.

DIFFERENT STROKES FOR DIFFERENT FOLKS. Up until this point we've been assuming that every positive incentive has an equal attraction to stimulate change. Now you and I both know that's just not so. One man's meat is another man's poison. Unless we know a person intimately, it's extremely tough to predict what will motivate him. For instance, why am I writing this book? Listed below are six different wants that have driven others like myself to go through the agony of trying to get a book in print. Which would you bet is the predominant force that's prodding me on?

1. The forty cents per copy royalty will help me put groceries on the table.
2. The printing of this book will give me job security in today's "publish or perish" college teaching market.
3. Publication will gain me admission to the close knit fraternity of Christian authors.
4. There's a personal sense of accomplishment and a public esteem which comes from having your ideas printed in black and white.
5. I feel a satisfaction in adding to the world's total body of knowledge and contributing to the field of literature.
6. I want to respond to what I believe is God's will.

Quite frankly, I'm not completely certain myself. We all have mixed motives and my guess is that each of these reasons holds some appeal for me. I'd like to say that responding to God's will is the primary motivation, but in all honesty I think the fourth item is the one that kicks me out of bed at five in the morning and sends me to the typewriter. Of course God can use any motivation for his glory. Handel wrote the *Messiah* for money.

I raise the question of my reason for writing to illustrate the point that various people are turned on by separate rewards. Or as the heading of this section says it, "Different strokes for different folks." But we need to make sense out of all these conflicting drives if we're ever going to be able to offer benefits which we know will affect someone else. I think the best help in making order out of this chaos comes from the work of Abraham Maslow. Maslow claims that all humans have the same basic set of needs. He arranges them in a hierarchical order like steps on a staircase.

The most basic needs are the physical ones—the need for food, water, warmth, sleep, etc. In this we're no different from animals. If we're deprived of these basic physical needs, we can indeed turn into raging beasts. Accounts of life in concentration camps confirm that humans are apt to focus their entire energies on food when they can't get it. Men place pin-ups of steak on the wall. They risk severe beatings and humiliation just for the chance of an extra scrap of bread. The man who is starving usually won't respond to matters of safety, truth, dignity, or even fear of hell. This is why the Christian in Bangladesh must speak to and meet the hunger needs of the people. A strange thing happens when a person's physical needs are satisfied, however. They no longer motivate him. A drive that's satisfied no longer drives. When a man is able to climb above the first step of physical need, a whole new set of desires comes into play on the second level.

The second step is our need for security. This involves physical and psychological safety. The political appeal for law and order is an attempt to tap into feelings of insecurity. Interestingly enough, Maslow—a Jewish social philosopher and psychologist—also includes religion on the security level. He sees our desire for God springing out of a fear of unseen threats both in this world and in the world to come. I think this is only partially true. A person who feels completely secure still can experience a need for God. As I understand the faith, Jesus Christ offers to meet the needs of a man no matter what level he's on. Keith Miller takes the same position in his book *The Becomers*.[12] In two fine chapters he explains Maslow's hierarchy and draws its implication for the church. In fact, I feel somewhat like a phony trying to briefly sketch the ground that he's covered so well. I heartily recommend that you read it.

The third step is our need to belong. After our prepotent needs for physical necessity and personal safety are adequately met, we desire nothing more than to love and be loved—to be an appreciated part of a group of other human beings. Maslow claims that this is where the action is for most Americans today. I think he's right. That's why a warm Christian fellowship will do more to bring others to Jesus Christ than all the doctrinal statements in the world. Don't get me wrong. I think it's vital that we seek to discover and proclaim the truth of God, but we also need to recognize that most people are attracted to people more than they are to principles.

What if it's been your good fortune to surmount these first three levels? You've had your physical needs, your drive for safety, and your desire for belonging all satisfied since childhood. What's the fourth step on Maslow's staircase? It's the need for esteem, and I find myself poised on this step. You'll catch more of this in the final chapter, but for now it's enough to point out that self-satisfaction and the esteem of others is the predominant reason I've taken pen in hand to write this book. If you'll flip back a few pages, you'll notice that the possible motivations for writing follow Maslow's scheme. The cash for food reason would spring out of a physical craving. The publish or perish justification would be fostered by a threat to job security. The fellowship of authors would attract me if I had an unmet need for affiliation. But as a matter of fact, none of these tugs on me as strongly as the need for achievement. Perhaps if everyone who reads this book sings its praise and sends rave notices to the publisher, my need for esteem will be satisfied and I can then concentrate on Maslow's fifth level!

The fifth and final plateau on the staircase is our need for self-actualization. This is really a catchall term for a number of desires—the quest of intellectual understanding, aesthetic enjoyment, self-expression, creativity, purpose in life, etc. According to Maslow, these lie dormant in most of us because we haven't yet satisfied the lower needs. Certainly one of the aims of the gospel is to free a man from these lower drives so that he can become all that he has the potential to be—all that God intended him to be. That's what this top landing on the staircase is all about.

Here's a diagram of the steps:

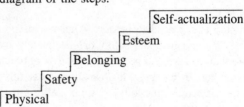

"I don't want a raise, Mr. Harlingen. I just want bouquets and accolades and tokens of esteem and bravos and huzzahs and a piece of the action."

On what level is the person you're trying to influence? Remember— none of this will do any good unless you can identify the need that's active in his life. Once you do, state the benefits of your plan for him that will help satisfy the need he's feeling. Don't aim too high—he's not even aware yet that he has those desires. Hopefully he will be later. Don't aim too low. Those things don't drive him anymore. Appeal to where he's at right now. If you can't honestly show him how your message will help meet that need, save your breath.

COKES AND CUTIES, BEEF AND BELLS. The whole thrust of the chapter so far has been to get you to think in terms of benefits. How will the attitude or action I want the other person to adopt bring benefit to him? Notice that this question implies a direct relationship between the incentive you offer and the action you want him to take. Save your back—use the dolly. Get stickers for your helmet—play better hockey. Here's a kernel of corn—walk in a figure eight. There's a whole host of rewards, however, that may have no logical connection with the person's response, yet are nevertheless powerful influencers.

A prime example is a commercial for Coca Cola. The ad shows a pretty girl drinking a Coke while a catchy song proclaims, "It's the real thing." What benefits are stated? None. But the average, red-blooded American male has to appreciate this cute gal. Her sex appeal has nothing to do with the taste of Coke, what it'll do for you, or to you. But the company hopes that some of the viewer's positive reaction toward the girl will spill over onto their product. The upbeat music doesn't hurt the product image either. This process is called "paired associative learning." The advertiser tries to get you to *learn* to *associate* together a *pair* of items—one of which you already like, the other their product.

Describing this linkage in words makes it sound like a ridiculous ploy. But it's actually quite persuasive. In the rest of the chapter I'm going to cite three experiments that show how forceful this kind of association can be. I'll conclude by showing the implications of this research for the Christian advocate.

Of course the classic study of paired association was performed by the Russian scientist Pavlov.[13] Pavlov would approach his laboratory dogs holding a hunk of meat. When they saw the meat and smelled its aroma, the dogs would salivate. Then Pavlov altered the procedure. He rang a bell at the same time he showed the meat, very much like presenting the girl and the Coke together. This didn't bother the dogs,

THROUGH HISTORY WITH J. WESLEY SMITH

"Do you mind if I go to lunch early, Professor Pavlov? I'm hungry."

their juices continued to flow. Finally one day Pavlov rang the bell without bringing the meat. The bell, which had no nutritional value, triggered the same response as the meat. Since the dogs had learned to mentally connect the bell with the meat, they slobbered all over the place. Thus Pavlov demonstrated that if two things are continuously linked together in time, we begin to assume that the one necessarily implies the other.

Paired association explains the findings of another experiment involving food.[14] In this study, the researcher had one group read a persuasive message while eating potato chips and pretzels. He also gave them a soft drink to quench their thirst. The other group read the same message without benefit of food. Those who ate while they read were more persuaded by the message than those who didn't. For most of us, eating is a gratifying pastime. We like it. Any ideas we happen to consider while we're eating benefit from the overall positive feeling that the food creates. I've always moaned about the excessive concern that church groups have with refreshments. It seems like we spend more time eating than meeting. This study suggests that the one helps the other.

I first read about the eating while reading experiment when I was in grad school. A group of us began to wonder if the warm glow from positive events would affect actions as well as attitudes. We decided to test out the possibility using compliments. We did this during the Christmas season in the downtown Chicago shopping area. We took turns standing alongside a woman at a stoplight and complimenting her appearance. We tried to select something about her that was genuinely attractive—her hair, her smile, the smartness of her coat, etc. We gave the compliment just before the light turned green and then headed off in a different direction. The reason for this was to avoid the impression that we had an ulterior or dishonorable motive in paying the compliment. All of this was done on the assumption that once she got over the surprise of being spoken to by a stranger, she'd feel good for having received some appreciation. About a hundred feet down the block there stood a Salvation Army worker ringing a bell, to collect money for needy children. We were able to casually observe who gave money and who passed on by without stopping. We predicted that women who received an unsolicited compliment would be more likely to contribute than women who didn't. And that's exactly what happened. Apparently "warm fuzzies" tend to make us more positive toward whatever appeal we hear.

What do Pavlov's dogs, eating while reading, and complimented women putting money in the kettle have to do with our witness for Jesus Christ? Just this—whether we like it or not, people are influenced not only by our message, but by the events which surround its presentation. The architecture of a church, the choir's anthem, and the time of day can all predispose church members to respond favorably to a pastor's sermon. Of course the opposite is also true. If we talk to someone about Jesus while we have bad breath, he learns to associate the Christian faith with something smelly and unpleasant. In this case it's not the gospel that's offensive, it's us.

We have a quality Lord! We need to present him to others in a quality manner. So often we settle for second-class when with a little effort we could have the best. In this regard I'm impressed by the high school summer camping program of Young Life. Every year over 10,000 kids spend a week considering the Savior amid a setting that's geared to be exciting and attractive to teenagers. Depending on which camp they go to, there's minibike racing, water skiing, mountain climbing, tennis, horseback riding and even a chance for a paraplane ride hundreds of feet in the air. The food is top-notch—steaks, roasts, chops, and chicken are standard fare. The entertainment is first-rate. For kids who usually think of camp as hunkering around a campfire with a can of beans, these places are truly teenage resorts. The kids' favorable response to the week carries over to their response to Jesus Christ.

Young Life gets a lot of static about their camps being too "plush." I think that this is because many Christians have adopted a missionary barrel mentality that says hand-me-downs are good enough for the Lord's work. Unfortunately this creates a smoggy atmosphere for our message. God calls us to be good stewards, but stewardship should be concerned with both sides of the minimax. Not only should we keep costs down, we need to offer quality benefits.

This whole discussion of paired association provides a good springboard into the topic of the next chapter. There's an inseparable bond between the message and the messenger. A speaker's credibility is going to affect how his message is received. As you read it, you might try to apply the concepts from the minimax to your own persuasive attempts. Are you a plus or a minus? Is your witness a benefit or a cost?

Credibility

My son had always hated mashed potatoes with a passion. We tried all the usual parental ploys to get him to eat them. Jeanie served tiny portions surrounded by foods he liked. She read stories while he took a taste every ten minutes or so. I tried a bribe of a different sort. I told him he'd have to wash the dishes if he didn't clean his plate. Jim decided that cleaning by washing was preferable to cleaning by eating.

Despite our failures, Jim now eats potatoes. How come? One night we had a college fellow named Don over to dinner. Don was a big, rugged, friendly guy. Jim especially admired him because he was captain and star of the soccer team. After dinner Don took Jim out in the backyard to kick a ball around. The next night Jim asked my wife to cook mashed potatoes. In response to her shocked expression he said simply, "Don says they're good for me."

This incident points up a central truth of persuasion—that *who* says something is just as important as *what* is said. For years I'd told Jim the exact same thing—that mashed potatoes would help make him strong. That message coming from me fell on deaf ears, but from the lips of Don it had persuasive impact. The messenger made the message. This idea is summed up in the old adage: "What you are speaks so loud I can't hear what you're saying.'' Persuasion rises or falls on the credibility of the speaker.

Obviously I'm not the first person in the world to discover the power of source credibility to sway an audience. Twenty-five hundred years ago Aristotle wrote the classic text on persuasion, *The Rhetoric*. He uses the Greek term *ethos* to describe the characteristics of a speaker that make his listeners want to believe him no matter what he says. He claims that ethos—ethical appeal—is the most important part of influence. If we believe we are listening to a good man, his cause will seem probable.

The Apostle Paul was quite aware of the effect ethos could have on winning others to the cause of Christ. From his own words we know that he made a conscious attempt to identify with those he sought to reach.

To the Jews I became as a Jew, in order to win Jews; to those under the law I became as one under the law . . .that I might win those under the law. To those outside the law I became as one outside the law . . .that I might win those outside the law. To the weak I became weak, that I might win the weak. I have become all things to all men, that I might by all means save some (1 Corinthians 9:20-22).

Nor was Paul concerned with his credibility only when he was around unbelievers. The last four chapters of 2 Corinthians is an extended appeal for the church to reexamine Paul's lifestyle as a messenger of God. His reluctant boasting touches upon his physical suffering, his love for the Corinthians, the fact that he didn't make a profit from preaching the gospel, and his direct vision of the resurrected Christ. He reminds his readers of this history in order to reestablish his authority as an apostle.

One of the first lessons I learned when I joined the staff of Young Life was that my credibility with high school kids would make or break the effectiveness of my witness. I quickly discovered that it took me fifteen to twenty hours a week to run a good club. The actual message preparation and direct counseling required only a few of those hours. But it took great gobs of time to demonstrate to them that I was an OK person who really cared about them. I did this by watching football practice on fall afternoons, going to sophomore cross-country meets, and attending school plays. It involved getting my hands dirty as I worked with a guy on his car and driving another fellow to a shopping center because he didn't have a car. It meant being willing to listen to rock music while sitting in the local Coke spot—engaged in the art of small talk about the world of dates, dances, and dragsters. I'm sure that to an outsider it looked like time wasted. After all, I was just hanging around—with no chance really to share the Christian faith. But I saw it as an indispensable way to win a hearing for my message. When I spoke to these kids about Jesus at our Tuesday night club meeting, I spoke not as an outsider, but as an adult friend who knew where they were at, and I'd already evidenced concern for them as individuals. In short—I had credibility.

I like to illustrate the importance of source credibility to students in my persuasion class by presenting a series of famous quotations. These are typical of statements I use:

1. *Give me four years to teach the children and the seed I have planted will never be uprooted.* (Mao Tse-tung)
2. *The fear of ideas makes us impotent and ineffective.* (Martin Luther)
3. *There is always room for a man of force and he makes room for many.* (Joseph Stalin)
4. *There is only one grade of men; they are all contemptible.* (Billy Graham)

You'll notice that each quote is attributed to a famous person. Actually the men above didn't say these things. In fact, while some students receive the form that links the statement about training children to Mao Tse-tung, others receive a different sheet that credits it to Martin Luther. After the students indicate the amount of agreement with each item, I ask the class if their attitude was affected by who stated the idea. Most students maintain that the source of the thought had no influence upon them, and many claim that they didn't even notice the man's name. Yet when we total up the overall results, we almost always find that there's much more agreement with the idea if it comes from Luther than if it originates with Mao Tse-tung.

This mini-experiment is not original with me. Thousands of similar studies have been run to probe the causes and effects of credibility.[15] Some of the results are rather esoteric and not particularly helpful for the practitioner of persuasion. Some of the findings, however, are central to an understanding of Christian influence. In the rest of the chapter I'll seek to answer five central questions about credibility. Specifically these are:

1. Does a speaker's credibility affect everyone the same way?
2. What are the different types of credibility?
3. Do the effects of credibility last over time?
4. Is a man's ethos fixed—written in stone—or can he alter it?
5. How can you improve your credibility in the eyes of those you want to reach?

IN THE EYE OF THE BEHOLDER. Our culture contains a number of truisms which reflect the fact that two people can react quite differently to the same stimulus person.

"Beauty is in the eye of the beholder."
"One man's meat is another man's poison."
"No man is a hero to his own valet."

These statements suggest that credibility isn't so much a personality trait possessed by a speaker as it is an aura of acceptance bestowed upon him by the listener. I recently heard a message by a man who evoked in me a response of complete trust. His whole mood and manner placed me at ease. I wanted to believe him. I was shocked to find out that the lady next to me had exactly the opposite reaction. At the end of the speech, she turned abruptly toward me and said through clenched teeth, "That man drives me up the wall. No matter what he says I want to scream out 'No!' "

I had a milder but similar reaction when I attended a Kathryn Kuhlman healing service. I tended to be skeptical of what she said and was put off by her methods. Not so the vast majority of the audience. Most had traveled hundreds of miles to attend. Although the service didn't start until 9:00 A.M., there were over 1,000 people standing outside the church in falling rain when I arrived at 4:00 A.M. As I talked to individuals while we waited, it became apparent that the crowd was made up of true believers—not only of the Lord, but of Miss Kuhlman as well. Some had experienced healing at previous meetings, while others were there because of the testimony of friends or relatives. The respect, trust, and near adulation they felt was visible during the four-hour service. It was obvious that Kathryn Kuhlman had fantastically high credibility with these people. They wanted to believe her. Yet I was watching the exact same performance and felt all sorts of doubts. I was viewing through critical glasses. The gap in our reactions made me realize once again that credibility is in the eye of the beholder.

If we need further evidence that a man's ethos can vary according to the judge, we need only look back at the first quotation on page 117. My class found it much more credible when it was attributed to Luther than when they thought it was voiced by Mao Tse-tung. But suppose the same attitude scale was presented not at a Christian college, but rather in Communist China? It doesn't take a prophet or the son of a prophet to predict that the credibility of Luther would plummet while the esteem for Chairman Mao would soar.

What all this means is that credibility is audience specific. Just because we've earned the respect of one group is no guarantee we'll be heard by another. This was brought home to me quite forcefully when I spoke to a group of junior high kids at a nearby church. Because of the time I've spent with high school fellows and gals, I've become accustomed to having a certain amount of clout when I speak in the community. I received a flowing introduction from the youth pastor and stepped up confidently to dispense my nuggets of wisdom. Were they impressed? No way! Within thirty seconds the place was up for grabs. They didn't know me from Adam and they saw no particular reason why they should listen with sympathetic ears. In fact, they obviously saw no reason to listen at all.

According to Jesus, there are places where a prophet is not honored. Credibility is in the eye of the beholder.

THE THREE FACES OF CREDIBILITY. I entered into the world of competitive swimming the summer before I started high school. Over the next six years I swam in 300 races and spent in excess of 100 total days in the water. During this time I worked under three different coaches. Each of them had a great influence on my swimming career. They were persuasive. When they spoke, I listened. They all possessed high credibility in my eyes, yet the reason for my high regard varied greatly from man to man. The nature of the credibility was different in each case.

Coach Moyle was a whirlwind of activity. It was he who spotted me that first summer as I lounged by the side of the pool. He walked briskly over and began to persuade me to join the club team. He claimed he could make me into a great swimmer. I was flattered. No outside adult had taken an avid interest in me before. He painted a picture of healthy exercise, friendship of other swimmers, and the ribbons, medals, and trophies that could be mine. It was impossible to say no to such an enthusiastic, outgoing person. His irresistible excitement continued throughout the summer. He planned special morning practices tailored just for me, took movies of my stroke, had me work out with a gal who was training for the Olympics, and called me the night before each meet to discuss strategy for the next day's race. We can label this facet of credibility dynamism, enthusiasm, responsiveness, or activity. Whatever we call it, Coach Moyle had it—and it made him a credible source.

In terms of energy, my high school coach was the exact opposite. Coach Tweedie was a slow-moving, hesitant man who never raised his voice. He didn't seem excited when we won or upset when we lost. Yet he had a cluster of character traits that gave him high ethos in my eyes. Coach Tweedie was a good man. He was honest and straightforward. In the four years I swam for him, I never saw him do anything devious or say a mean word. High school kids can be quite cruel to each other, so he took great pains to insure that no member of the team would be hurt by the thoughtless words of others. He was interested in me as a person. He'd often stay after practice and ask about my studies, family, or date life. After I became a Christian, he was willing to share his own beliefs and express his inner doubts. He didn't pretend to know much about the technique of swimming—he was a gym teacher assigned to coach the team. But because of his personal warmth and integrity, I worked hard for the man. We can call this aspect of credibility character, trustworthiness, or safety. Coach Tweedie inspired confidence because he appeared to be without guile.

"I see our next speaker needs no introduction. . . ."

If my high school coach radiated warmth, my college coach struck me as a cold fish. He seemed distant and aloof. He spoke to me individually only once or twice a week. Yet when he did deign to give me advice, I hung on every word. The reason was simple—Coach Steiger knew more about competitive swimming than everyone else I'd met put together. In ten seconds he could spot what I was doing wrong. What's more, he could tell me clearly and precisely how to correct the problem. In the sport of swimming, Coach Steiger was authoritative, intelligent, competent, and qualified. These terms describe the third aspect of ethos.

I've spoken of these three components as if they're mutually exclusive. They're not. It's quite possible for someone to be regarded as authoritative, trustworthy, and dynamic all at the same time. The man who possesses this kind of charisma obviously has a huge head start in the race to influence. People want to believe him. He has only to state his case. Unless he suggests something patently ridiculous or offensive, attitudes and actions will change.

How's your credibility? If you're reading this book, the chances are you're interested in influencing someone—or a lot of someones—for

Jesus Christ. How do they view you? You might want to use the credibility checklist on this and the next page to check it out. The first six pairs of words tap into the issue of authoritativeness or competence. The next batch deal with character or trustworthiness. And the final list is concerned with dynamism or responsiveness. If the people you're trying to reach would mark you on the far left for most items, you're well on the way to being an agent of change. If they'd repeatedly tend to place a check toward the right, some soul-searching and fence mending are in order.

AUTHORITATIVENESS

Qualified	:___:___:___:___:___:___:	Unqualified
Expert	:___:___:___:___:___:___:	Inexpert
Informed	:___:___:___:___:___:___:	Uninformed
Intelligent	:___:___:___:___:___:___:	Unintelligent
Trained	:___:___:___:___:___:___:	Untrained
Reliable	:___:___:___:___:___:___:	Unreliable

CHARACTER

Friendly	:___:___:___:___:___:___:	Unfriendly
Kind	:___:___:___:___:___:___:	Cruel
Just	:___:___:___:___:___:___:	Unjust
Unselfish	:___:___:___:___:___:___:	Selfish
Pleasant	:___:___:___:___:___:___:	Unpleasant
Honest	:___:___:___:___:___:___:	Dishonest

DYNAMISM

Active	:___:___:___:___:___:___:	Passive
Open	:___:___:___:___:___:___:	Closed
Bold	:___:___:___:___:___:___:	Timid
Cheerful	:___:___:___:___:___:___:	Gloomy
Emphatic	:___:___:___:___:___:___:	Hesitant
Responsive	:___:___:___:___:___:___:	Unresponsive

SLEEPER EFFECT. In the opening chapter I stated that persuasion is trivial if it doesn't last over time. It doesn't do any good when we convince a man only for a season. If he reverts back, he'll just become more set in that original opinion. As Jesus notes in the parable of the empty house, "The last state of that man is worse than the first."

This is the "Achilles' heel" of credibility. Although people are easily swayed by the charismatic speaker or the winsome counselor, the change is often short-lived. In fact some research shows that a message coming from the mouth of a person with low ethos may be just as persuasive *over time* as it is coming from a highly regarded source.

One study presented messages about a number of different topics to college men and women.[16] Some of the speeches were attributed to highly credible experts while others were linked to people you wouldn't expect to know much about the issue. For instance, a high ethos source talking about a cure for the common cold might be the chief research physician at the National Institute for Health. Students exposed to the low credibility condition would hear the same message, but be told that it was delivered by a high school sophomore in his speech class. At first there was a great difference in reaction. On a scale of one to 100, those who thought it came from a high ethos source changed a whopping twenty-three percent, while those who heard the low ethos source changed only six percent. But this difference had completely disappeared when the participants were questioned one month later.

The graph below shows the surprising way this happened. Nearly half of the original attitude change produced by the high ethos speaker was washed out after four weeks. But the strange thing was that the folks who heard the low ethos source showed more change after four weeks than they did originally.

This sort of thing happens often enough so that it's come to be called by a special name—the "sleeper effect." It's as if an audience is unimpressed by the words of the person who hasn't proven himself to be competent, safe, and responsive. But the message lies dormant in their minds and over time it arouses a new appreciation of the idea they initially rejected. Hence the term "sleeper effect."

There are two explanations for the "sleeper effect," and both of them give us a clue as to how the Christian persuader can maintain the positive benefits produced by high credibility. Let's consider what goes on in a person's mind when he hears a new idea. If the message comes from a "good guy," he feels he can relax. Surely a man as good as this wouldn't say anything wrong or harmful. So the idea is accepted without critical examination. He sees it through rose-colored glasses. But as time goes by, our friend may forget where he heard the idea. He's lost his cue as to how to interpret the message, so he reexamines it with critical eyes. He finds it doesn't look quite so good when viewed in this new harsh light. The reverse thing happens when the message comes from a "bad guy." The listener tosses up all sorts of resistance because he doesn't trust the speaker. After a while, though, he forgets who sponsored the thought and comes under the influence of the idea itself.

Put these reactions together and we see that credibility is a force over time only when the message and the source are inseparably linked in the mind of the hearer. Billy Graham does this well. His converts receive continuous follow-up from the association that bears his name. Whenever they think of Billy Graham, they automatically are reminded of his message. As long as they continue to admire Billy, they'll approve his gospel. There's nothing shady about this. Paul made a direct invitation to those who admired him to identify with his devotion to the Lord. "Be imitators of me as I am of Christ."

The second contributing cause for the "sleeper effect" is the difference in cognitive work—the amount of mental exercise. You'll recall from Chapter 7, "Role Play," that active participation promotes persuasion. Consider our friend who's listening to a good guy. He's relaxed. He feels no need to mull over the idea. It's coming from an OK person, so it's OK too. He may not even remember it a few days later. Not so with the message that comes from a questionable source. He'll spend a great deal of mental energy to question it and look for flaws.

Although this results in initial rejection, the seed of an idea is planted and it may sprout over time. The moral is clear. The words of a highly respected person may be accepted so easily that they have no real impact. The effects of credibility continue only when the message is tasted, chewed, and digested. If it's gulped down whole, it'll have no lasting effect.

What all this means is that when we talk about Jesus Christ, we've got to make sure that people focus on the message, not the messenger. Now I'm sure we agree with this in theory. But when others look up to us, it's easy to get sucked into an ego trip. We naturally crave positive strokes. It feels great when we're surrounded by others who have confidence in our judgment and approve of our personality. It's a heady experience to have another human being come to us for guidance and counsel. And there's nothing quite so affirming as speaking to a group in which every face is gazing up in rapt attention—waiting to agree with whatever we say. But we need to be careful not to play up our own importance. If we fall into this trap, people will concentrate on us rather than on the truth we proclaim. They'll accept our thoughts without thinking much about them. And that's the problem—they'll be our thoughts, not theirs.

A HERO TODAY, A BUM TOMORROW. We've been talking about credibility as if it were a fixed entity—something you either have or you don't. Nothing could be further from the truth. A man's credibility with a given audience is constantly changing. It can go up and down like a yo-yo. Consider my view of Senator Mark Hatfield of Oregon. Hatfield has long been my favorite politician. He's honest, says what he believes, and has an engaging sense of humor. He took an early stand against American involvement in Viet Nam and has championed legislation to feed the hungry. As a Christian, he articulates his faith in a modest and winsome way. To me, he is a highly credible source. (Incidentally, don't be put off if you don't share my judgment of Hatfield. If you react differently to the man, it just shows what we've said all along—that credibility is in the eye of the beholder.)

I heard Hatfield speak two years ago. In his address he recommended that the United States cut back its aid to Israel. Hearing this was like a kick in the teeth. I'd always applauded our nation's role in helping

Israel survive while surrounded by hostile countries. Now I was in a quandary. Here was a man I liked recommending an action I didn't like. How was I going to resolve this inconsistency? I did it by making mental adjustments in my views both toward Israel and Hatfield. It's as if both attitudes were at opposite ends of a stretched rubber band. I reduced the tension by pulling them both toward the center. Thus aid to Israel has become suspect in my mind. I no longer give a knee-jerk type response of approval every time the issue comes up. But the speech modified my opinion of Hatfield as well. By taking this stand, he lost some of the credibility I'd ascribed to him. It's important to realize that this new level of credibility wasn't written in stone either. Since that time I've heard things about Hatfield that have lifted him back up higher than he was before the speech.

We can think of credibility as a bank account. A man builds up credit through his words and deeds which meet with others' approval. These deposits increase his potential to persuade. He can spend some of this acceptance capital in order to convince others. But if he keeps spending and spending without acquiring new resources, he'll go bankrupt—he'll use up all his credibility. At this point we cease to believe him or take seriously what he says. It's even possible through deficit spending to get into a position of negative credibility. In this case, we react just the opposite of what the person wants. His words drive us away. If he's for it—we're against it.

So we see that credibility is an ever-changing fluid commodity. This has a number of implications for the Christian persuader. It means we can never sit back on our haunches and think we have it made. As I pointed out at the start of the chapter, even Paul found it necessary to work at maintaining his ethos with the Christians at Corinth. It also means we shouldn't make a big deal out of every disagreement we have with others. It's possible to lose our credibility over numerous minor issues, and not have any left to draw on when something really important comes up. I know a Christian who argued with his next door neighbor about his leaf raking practices, fluoridation of water, the local school board election, and how to raise their children. When he had a chance to talk about what was really important to him—his faith in Jesus Christ—his reputation as a crabby reactionary blunted the force of his witness. Finally, we need to realize that like money, credibility is only valuable when it's used for something. It does no good to constantly work at building up our image if we never take a stand. Some issues are so vital that we've got to be willing to put it all on the line in an attempt to sway others.

WHAT YOUR DOG SAYS ABOUT YOU. Where have we come so far? I opened with the idea that a person's ethos varies depending on who's listening to him. I then stated that the listener makes judgments on the speaker's competence, trustworthiness, and energy level. I showed that the positive effects of credibility are short-lived unless the listener keeps calling to mind the speaker, and mentally wrestles with message content. Finally I suggested that credibility is constantly changing. All of this leads us to the crucial question about ethos: What can we do to raise our credibility?

The answer is—most anything. Everything we do or say affects how others judge our ideas—even the kind of dog we own.

There's an old saying that a man is known by the company he keeps. I once had two graduate students who set out to prove that a man's credibility is affected by the breed of canine he keeps in his home.[17] I thought the whole thing was ridiculous until I saw their results. They were concerned specifically with status, a measure akin to authoritativeness. They predicted that being seen with a low status dog would lower his social standing, but that ownership of a high status animal would gain him esteem.

They began their study by showing pictures of twelve different breeds to a large audience. The members rated their impression of each dog just as they might judge the varied status of cars like a Mercedes, Cadillac Seville, Dodge Charger, AMC Gremlin, or VW bug. My students found that some dogs were ranked consistently high: French poodle, Irish wolfhound, and Saint Bernard. Other dogs were at the bottom of the list: fox terrier and basset hound. (Bowser, our basset, has looked sad ever since hearing these findings.)

These fellows then showed slides of men at work to a similar but different audience. This group marked down how they viewed the status of the workers. Doctors, computer scientists, and airline pilots scored high. Garbage collectors, gardeners, and commercial fishermen were at the low end of the totem pole.

"I'm afraid it would ruin my image as a humble servant to mankind."

Finally the two young researchers paired the dogs with the men for a third audience. They systematically rotated things around so that high status dogs were shown with low status men and vice versa. Their instructions led the audience to assume that they were seeing pictures of twelve different men posing with the family pet. The status ratings confirmed the students' initial hunch. In eleven out of twelve cases, the perceived status of the workers shifted in the direction of the dog he owned. For instance, a construction worker who was judged to have relatively low status came up in the world when seen with a Saint Bernard. The reverse was also true. A common fox terrier hurt the image of the computer technician. (Basset hound owners beware! Your dog is pulling you down.)

Now please don't rush out to your local kennel to trade in the family mutt for a pedigreed Irish wolfhound. I doubt whether it would aid you in attracting people into the kingdom of God. But that's not the point. I've presented this material in order to highlight the fact that even a seemingly trivial item can affect the confidence with which others view our beliefs. If the type of dog we own has some influence, think how much more impact our disposition, the manner in which we handle money, or the way we treat our kids has upon people as they judge the sincerity of our faith.

It's impossible to draw up a definitive list of ways to hypo your credibility. However the following suggestions have stood the test of time as methods which will win a hearing for your words.

To increase authoritativeness—Actually know what you're talking about. I once heard a sermon on Elijah's contest with the prophets of Baal. The minister claimed that the fire from heaven was the first recorded case in history of an atomic chain reaction. His references to nuclear fusion made it clear that he didn't know an atom from Adam. He therefore lost the respect of his audience. It may take further schooling, private study, or practical experience, but make sure you actually possess some expertise.

Find points of agreement between you and your hearers. We're all human. We tend to think that anyone who agrees with us is a rather astute and clever thinker. Don't bluff. You may disagree with them in starting point, method, and conclusion; but if you can honestly discover common areas of agreement, point them out.

Be organized! The world questions the competence of a man who beats around the bush, stumbles over his words, and intersperses "and ums" into his speech. A clear and concise statement of what you believe carries weight.

Get an introduction from a credible source. Ethos can be transferred to a certain extent. The sponsorship of an intelligent and accepted group member can give a real boost to your opening words.

To increase trustworthiness—Spend lots of time with those you wish to influence. There's a line from an old show tune that goes, "When I'm not near the one I love, I love the one I'm near." This sentiment reveals a noticeable lack of commitment, but it also reflects a fact of life. Deep trust requires long-run proximity. The more we're around the other person, the better chance there is he'll regard us as a good man.

Don't lie, don't gossip, don't cut others down. James was right when he said the tongue can set a forest ablaze, and there's a real temptation to be verbal pyromaniacs. It's easy to draw a crowd if we're willing to

"Make me soft and cuddly."

bend the truth, spill a confidence, or take a cheap shot at another human being. But even though an audience might show outward glee, they're mentally filing away evidence that we're not to be trusted.

Engage in the difficult task of self-disclosure. James says, "Get into the habit of admitting your sins to each other" (James 5:15, *Phillips*). This is the most ignored bit of advice I know of in Scripture, probably because we're afraid that people won't like us or trust us when they see how crummy we really are. But the reverse is true. They've got the same sin problem. As we openly reveal our innermost struggles, the plastic masks we wear begin to slip. Human warmth escapes and people begin to respond in trust.

If you want someone to trust you, trust them. I know this sounds risky. It is! But going around like Eeyore the donkey in *Winnie the Pooh*—gloomy and expecting the worst from everybody—is a surefire way of arousing defensiveness. I'd rather be like the turtle who makes progress only when he sticks out his neck. Trust breeds trust.

To increase dynamism—Be enthusiastic! "Whatever your hand finds to do, do it with your might" (Ecclesiastes 9:10). Jesus chastised the early church of Laodicea because they were lukewarm. We too live in an age of "casual coolness" where many people appear just to go through the motions. A genuine excitement about what you believe will stand out in bold relief. Enthusiasm is contagious.

Be different. Try something new. Change your approach from time to time. One of the deadening things about many church services is that they're so predictable. People reach for their wallets during the prayer because they know the offering is next. While the collection plate is passed, they pull out the hymnal because they know the singing comes next. It always has! The man who sticks to the routine appears dull. When he breaks out and does the unexpected, we see him as a mover.

* * * *

This chapter has focused on the messenger. We've seen that the man behind the words plays a crucial role in whether or not they mold the audience. Credibility wins a hearing. It even makes others *want* to believe the message. But the words themselves make a difference as well. Now we need to look at how to present the message itself. That's the next chapter.

10

Presenting the Message

Now how can they call on one in whom they have never believed? How can they believe in one of whom they have never heard? . . .(Belief, you see, can only come from hearing the message, and the message is the word of Christ.) (Romans 10:14, 17, Phillips).

Paul had a story to tell—the Jesus story. He'd long ago decided that he'd stick to the basics: Jesus died on a cross for our sins just as the Scriptures had prophesied. Jesus was buried, but the grave couldn't hold him. On the third day, he was raised to life and appeared to many different people, including Paul. Paul knew he had a story to tell, but how best to tell it?

That's what this chapter is about. I'm assuming you have a story to tell. The fact that you've gotten this far into the book suggests that you're committed to certain truths about God which you want to share with others. So the question isn't so much *what* to say as *how* to say it. As a speech teacher, I hear an average of 500 speeches a year. I've had the continual opportunity to observe what makes the face of a listener light up in understanding, and what produces a frown of confusion. I've had the chance to check out the things that turn an audience on, and I've seen what drives them away. These conclusions coupled with the research findings of communication studies have led me to the specific advice contained in this chapter.

You'll notice that the message suggestions I make are slanted toward a public speaking situation. That's because the bulk of message research has been done in a speaker-audience setting. But don't be put off if your interest runs more along the lines of a one-on-one interpersonal dialogue. The principles that make for an effective congregational sermon can also be applied to telling a bedtime Bible story to your daughter or sharing your faith with a friend at the office.

TELEGRAPHING THE PUNCH. Aristotle said that all the persuasive speaker had to do was state his case and prove it. You'd think the first part of that task would be easy—but not so. I was reminded how tough it is when I sent a telegram to my representative about a food assistance bill before Congress. The fact that I'm a voter in his district gave my message a certain amount of clout, but I had to sum up my thoughts in a short space in order to sway him. It was excruciatingly difficult to state my main point in ten to fifteen words. You may find it equally hard to cast all of your ideas in one simple declarative sentence, but it's a discipline I strongly recommend whenever you speak. It's necessary because we ordinarily tend to hem and haw, toss in lots of verbal filler, and rob our ideas of power by using cop-out qualifiers like sort of, kind of, perhaps, rather, and maybe. When we finally do finish, we aren't sure at all that what we've said is what we actually meant. And our audience isn't even certain what we've said. For both their sake and ours, we need to present our main thrust in a single line.

Is it wise to present this main point at the start of the message, or would we be better off to wait until the conclusion? We'd do well to follow the advice of a successful country preacher. When asked the secret of his success he replied, "It's simple. I tell them what I'm going to say. I say it. Then I tell them what I've said." Let people know where you're headed right from the start. This way they'll have a mental hook on which to hang all the illustrations and evidence you can muster to support your thesis. If they don't know where you're headed, they might unconciously twist an example you give and see it as bolstering a different point of view.

There's only one time that it's wise to hold back on presenting your

"Now that we've learned to talk, let's not speak in vague generalities."

opinion right from the start. That's when you expect the audience to be hostile to your position. Suppose you're advocating compulsory gun registration to a group of hunters at a National Rifle Association meeting. (Good luck!) If you state your conclusion at the start, they'll shout you down or laugh you out before you have a chance to support your position. Probably nothing's going to work. But at least you've got a chance if you work inductively from your support evidence. Build your case slowly by presenting facts, quotes from respected sources, examples, and lines of argument. Finally at the end you come to your conclusion by saying, "Therefore . . ." and you present the main idea.

How often should the main point be restated? Are one or two times enough or do we need to spell it out repeatedly? It's quite possible that our audience could grasp our conclusion with only one or two restatements. But the important issue is whether or not they'll remember it at some later date. It's reasonable to assume that there will be some forgetting over time. I find I can't always remember what I spoke on myself, much less recall what someone else said. This forgetfulness could be crucial, because long-lasting attitude change is strongly connected to remembering the thesis of the message. We don't need to sweat the details, but our audience has to recall our main thrust or there will be no persuasion over time. That's one reason I've placed such a strong emphasis on the art of distilling your ideas into a single memorable sentence.

We need therefore to stimulate our hearers to "overlearn" our conclusion when we speak. If we can accomplish this, they'll still remember our main point long after they've forgotten most of what we've said. Overlearning comes through repetition. Six to eight restatements of the conclusion in a twenty-minute speech is not too much. Of course we run the risk of appearing too simplistic by belaboring the obvious— but it's a chance well worth taking. Unless our main point becomes thoroughly ingrained in the minds of our audience, we'll have no lasting influence.

Even if we boil down our thoughts into one succinct phrase and restate it often, there's no guarantee that our audience will really catch what we have in mind. There's an old story about three umpires who were talking shop. The first umpire said, "Some are balls, some are strikes. I calls them as they is." The second umpire wasn't so sure. He

"He had this dirty bumper sticker on his car. It said
ESCHEW OBFUSCATION."

put it this way. "Some are balls, some are strikes. I call 'em as I see 'em." The third umpire felt the need to correct them both. He flatly declared, "Some are balls and some are strikes, but they ain't nothing 'till I calls them." The same is true with words. Words don't mean things, people mean things. And there's always the chance that the words we select to present our main point may mean something very different to our hearers than they do to us. That's why it's wise to state our case in two or three different ways. If the first one fogs by some of our listeners, the second or third blend of words may click in as we intended.

I've stressed the importance of working hard to get across a main point. Is it possible that after all our precautions the audience will understand exactly what we have in mind, and yet be repelled by the idea? Can the mere statement of our opinion drive them away? The answer is yes. Every man is tolerant only up to a point. There's a range of opinion on either side of his position that he'll at least consider. Psychologists call this region the "latitude of acceptance." When he hears a message that falls within these limits, there's a good chance he'll be swayed by the appeal. Outside these limits lies his "latitude of rejection." Ideas within these areas will strike him as "far out," and he'll automatically reject them. In fact, they may even trigger a boomerang effect and drive him farther away.

Let me illustrate the latitude idea with the example I used before—advocating gun control to the National Rifle Association. The diagram following is a mental map of the typical NRA member concerning gun regulation. From this you can see that it would be fruitless to approach him suggesting the registration of all firearms. That's well outside his latitude of acceptance. The mere thought would turn him off. On the other hand, he might be willing to consider an import ban on the cheap "Saturday night specials." That's not where he's at, but at least it's a legitimate option for him. If you did get him to move this far, his latitude of acceptance would shift slightly leftward to the point where he might be open to the idea of handgun registration.

The whole latitude idea is akin to the melting-molding model presented in Chapter 1. Melting can be seen as the process of extending another's latitude of acceptance. Molding takes place only when the message falls within that latitude. The implication is obvious. It serves

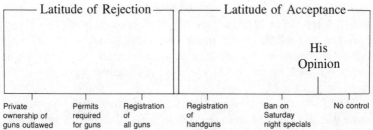

Latitude of Rejection			Latitude of Acceptance		
				His Opinion	
Private ownership of guns outlawed	Permits required for guns	Registration of all guns	Registration of handguns	Ban on Saturday night specials	No control

little purpose to bomb another with an idea that's squarely within his latitude of rejection. The Apostle Peter recognized this when he advocated the spiritual milk of God's Word for young Christians. They would have choked on meaty chunks. In other words, persuasion—like Christian growth—is a gradual process.

SPEAKING IN PICTURES. Our family spends part of each summer on a remote island in Lake Michigan. We're completely out of touch with the rest of the world—there's no one else on the island, no phone, and the nearest people are ten miles away over water. This kind of temporary isolation has many advantages. Since there's no TV, we get in plenty of reading. We share all work jointly and this promotes family solidarity. There's no ironclad schedule to follow or interruptions to distract us when we get caught up in a pet project. There is one large potential drawback however—safety. Jeanie and I are quite concerned that we be able to call in medical help fast in case of emergency.

I purchased a VHF radio transceiver to cover this possibility. I thought it wise to train the kids to use it on the off chance that Jeanie and I were out of commission at the same time. One morning I showed them how to hook up the battery, tune to the proper frequency, and key the microphone. Sharon said she understood all that, but didn't know what to say once you got on the air. I told her that the universal distress call was "Mayday, mayday."

In the afternoon we all went swimming. When Jeanie came shivering out of the cold water, Sharon pointed to the bumps on her legs and said, "Oooh, what are those ugly things?" Jeanie laughed and told her they were called goose pimples.

That night Sharon started playing the "what if" game. "Dad, what if we were up here during the winter and you and Mom fell through the

ice? What should I do?'' Having just read a book on nondirective counseling, I decided to let her answer her own question. In my best Roge-
rian manner I asked, ''What *would* you do?'' A look of proud confidence came upon her face as she eagerly announced: ''I'd dash over to
the radio, pick up the mike, and say, 'Springtime, springtime, my
mom has duck dots.' ''

Think about it. She wasn't that far off, was she? Mayday →
Springtime. Goose pimples → Duck dots. Notice that my words
triggered pictures in Sharon's mind. This is typical. We don't think in
abstractions, we think in pictures. Sharon forgot the words, but she
caught the imagery.

Pictures in the mind move people. We know that one picture is worth
a thousand words, but we often forget that we can use words to paint
powerful mental images. I remember once when I was ten years old
listening to a radio drama of H. G. Wells' *The Time Machine*. Since it
was well past my bedtime, I lay in the dark with the radio turned low. I
grew tense as the narrator described the underground world of the future. After a while I became so scared that I reached out and turned off
the radio. But the images which the words had fostered wouldn't go
away. Instead they continued to build. I finally had to turn the radio
back on in order to dispel the terrifying scene my mind had created.
Pictorial words have power.

Our Lord knew this. He spoke in parables. Some students of Scripture claim he did this to be evasive. But the effect was persuasive. In
their mind's eye his hearers saw the joy on the face of the father when
his prodigal son returned—and they grasped the forgiveness of God the
Father. When it comes down to a contest between a storyteller and a
didactic preacher, the storyteller will carry the day every time.

My specific advice for you is to use words that help your listener call
up in his mind the same image that you have in yours. Don't just talk
about the power of God in the abstract. Who knows what he'll picture if
you leave it that vague? Use a specific example as a springboard. Talk
about Christ stilling the waves as reported in Mark 4. Get him to visualize the small boat plunging down the backside of a twenty-foot
wave. Get him to see the desperation on the disciples' faces as they
scream, ''Master, don't you care that we're drowning?'' Stimulate his
other senses as well. Encourage him to hear the roar of a forty-mph

"... You turn left, make a right, then left and left again, then go right, left, right ..."

gale that snatches away every yell. Get him to feel the numbing ache of muscles straining against the oars—the sting of salt spray in the membrane of the eyes and nose. Then contrast this chaos with the dead calm which followed Jesus' command. If you get the listener to mentally place himself in this situation, he'll gain a new appreciation of Christ's power.

I've tried to practice what I preach in writing this book. The only effective way for me to communicate new material is by analogy—comparing the ideas and illustrating them with things you already know. Ideally I'd do this by referring to some common experience we've had together. But since I can't be sure we've had the same past experience, the next best way is to create new common ground as I write. That's why I've already exposed you to Sharon's candle-making efforts, my attitude toward dogs, my childhood fear of falling into Tampa Bay, my relationship with my father, swim coaches I have known, and my experience coaching a boys' hockey team. For the same reason you'll read in later chapters about my children watching TV in a Niagara Falls motel, the attractive group of kids who introduced me to Jesus Christ, and Jeanie's frustration with an absentee husband. I'm not just ego-tripping when I sketch these scenes—although I'm quite aware that like everyone else I have a deep desire to be known by others. But I've discovered that a message requires vivid illustrations and personal examples in order to be persuasive.

In all fairness I should point out that not everyone agrees with me. I submitted the first seven chapters of this manuscript to several publishers to see if I was writing something worth printing. One editor responded by saying he thought that the principles I presented were quite valuable, but that the many stories and personal references detracted from the material. If I wanted to write an academically respectable book, he said, I'd have to cut out the bulk of the illustrations. Obviously, I've ignored his advice and taken the book elsewhere. I'm committed to the proposition that pictures persuade. You'll have to decide who's right.

THE HEAD VS. THE HEART. Sometime in the earth's distant past there was an unnamed caveman who decided he'd try to convince with words rather than coerce with a club. Ever since that time men have tended to divide persuasive appeals into two categories which seem mutually exclusive—emotional and rational. Some persuaders emphasize man's similarity with other animals and they favor the emotional approach. Other advocates stress man's ability to think and therefore champion the rational approach. As for me, I think it's a false dichotomy. I don't see them as opposite. I've heard fine speeches that contain both strong sentiment and strong logic. Unfortunately I've heard many more that were neither emotional nor rational. As bread cast upon the water, they just sogged and sank.

I choose to think of these two appeals as complementary—both necessary for a successful message. Emotions are what move us—logic tells us which direction to go. Feelings show us our need—rational thoughts suggest solutions to meet that need. Emotions are drive inducing, they turn us on. Rational discourse is drive reducing; it calms us down. Believing as I do that a truly persuasive message will speak to both feelings and intellect, I'll use the rest of the chapter to describe methods of enhancing both appeals. Let's deal with emotions first.

To be human is to want. All of us have unmet needs and desires, although they vary from person to person. Some humans are hungry and want food, others are lonely and crave companionship. There are those who are scared and desire peace, and those who are frustrated and demand freedom. The goal of many is to achieve success while others seek the assurance that their life has eternal meaning. Any message that taps into one of these unfulfilled longings is emotional. You can draw a gut level response by talking about things that really matter to your audience.

Another effective way to evoke an emotional response is to display that reaction yourself. We tend to rejoice with those who rejoice and weep with those who weep. An audience will usually pick up the mood of the speaker. If he's excited, so are they. If he appears bored, however, the audience will mentally check out even if they remain physically present in their seats. Emotions are communicated mainly through nonverbal channels. Facial expression is most important, and tone of voice is a close second. If the words tell one story and the face and voice report another, the audience will believe the nonverbal cues every time. That's why it's important to let your words affect you as well as your hearers. A detached stance, lack of eye contact, and a monotone voice rob words of their emotional impact.

Along this line I strongly advise against writing out a speech ahead of time. It's true that a manuscript keeps you from forgetting what you want to say, but what you gain in certainty is more than offset by the way it affects the mood of the audience. In the first place, very few of us write the way we talk. Something happens when we take pen in hand—we try to polish up our everyday speaking habits, doing away with common slang and contractions. The result is often a stilted, formal prose that sounds suspiciously like a textbook. Even if we do manage to write as we talk, we have a tough time reading as we talk. Our voice is flat and expressionless, the rate uniform. Our eyes are on the page, our face is hidden from view. (If you feel I'm exaggerating the difficulty, check out how the liturgist reads the Scripture lesson in your next worship service.) Finally there's a problem of perceived sincerity. Somehow the guy who speaks to us directly without copious notes seems to mean what he says. We're a bit suspicious though of the speaker who resorts to a prepared text. It may not be fair, but listeners question whether a speaker really believes his own words if he has to write them down first. So don't write out your message!

If you take this advice seriously, you may open yourself up to the danger of unorganized rambling. Be careful, for nothing turns an audience off faster than going too long. Jim Rayburn, the founder of Young Life, used to say that it's a sin to bore people when talking about Jesus Christ. I believe it. The man who misses a number of good stopping points is in danger of sin. It's hard to squeeze all of your thoughts into a narrow time slot. It's much easier to ramble. Mark Twain once wrote a friend and put it this way: "Please forgive me for writing such a long letter. I didn't have time to write a short one." Being flexible without being sloppy is a tough balance. It's worth striving for, though, because the combination ensures maximum emotional impact.

Emotion is vital to persuasion, but most public speakers would agree that this is only part of the story. Take trial lawyers for example. They see their job as twofold: 1) To bring the jury to the point where they *want* to decide favorably—these are matters of the heart; and 2) To make it *reasonable* for them to do so—these are matters of the head. Now let's shift our attention to the second task. What makes a message reasonable to an audience?

The answer is evidence. In order to win them over to your point of view, you have to assemble evidence that will cause them to conclude beyond reasonable doubt that your position is sound. As they listen to your plea, an audience is constantly asking three things about your evidence:

Is it true?
Is it the whole truth?
What does it have to do with the issues at hand?

Suppose you're asked to speak to a church group on the topic of judgment. The leaders are concerned that petty criticisms are driving away possible new members. They're hoping you can say something to alter this backbiting trend. Your main point is that members of the congregation should quit judging each other's behavior. To support your idea you quote from Paul's famous passage on judgment.

"Why, then, criticise your brother's actions, why try to make him look small? We shall all be judged one day, not by each other's standards or even by our own, but by the judgment of God . . .It is to God alone that we have to answer for our actions. Let us therefore stop turning critical eyes on one another. If we must be critical, let us be critical of our own conduct and see that we do nothing to make a brother stumble or fall" (Romans 14:10-13, *Phillips*).

This is one piece of evidence. How will it hold up? It will convince only to the extent that your hearers are satisfied with your answers to these three questions.

"Is it true?" Chances are that most of the congregation already accepts the validity of the Bible. They'll consider evidence from God's Word as true, unless they quibble with the particular translation. If they do question Phillips' version, you'd better be ready to quote from the RSV, *New English Bible*, or King James—whichever they regard as most reliable. For those who don't accept the authority of Scripture, you'll either have to convince them that it's divine revelation or include extrabiblical evidence as well. Otherwise your message will stumble over the hurdle of perceived truth.

"Is it the whole truth?" Audiences are suspicious that we'll tell them only part of the story, the part that's favorable to our side. A listener who examines your Romans 14 evidence may say, "Yes, but what about 1 Corinthians 5? Doesn't Paul pronounce judgment on a man's action in the name of the Lord and then commit him to Satan?" You need to anticipate that question and show that Romans 14 is not an isolated proof text—that an ethic of nonjudgment is found consistently throughout the Bible. Don't fall into the trap of ignoring opposing viewpoints. Most audiences are smart enough to know there's two sides to every story. If there weren't some measure of doubt concerning your main point, why would you be trying to persuade them in the first place? It's better to deal openly with both sides of an issue and show that your evidence is representative of a whole body of supporting facts.

"What does all this have to do with the issue at hand?" You may have hearers who are willing to grant the truth of Romans 14, but believe that it's limited only to judgment of saints already within the fellowship. They may continue to criticize the faith and practice of those seeking to join the church. These folks take the position that your evidence isn't relevant to what they're doing. You have to show them that it is.

By this time you may be getting discouraged and conclude that nothing will ever sway the congregation—and you might well be right. Remember that you can't persuade someone if he doesn't want to change. As the old proverb says, "You can lead a horse to water but you can't make him drink." But this discussion of making your message rational has assumed you have a thirsty horse. If you do, you can do a lot to show him that your water is pure, that there's plenty more where it came from, and that it'll quench his thirst.

* * * *

In this chapter I've tried to touch base with the crucial areas of presenting a message. I've emphasized the importance of stating a specific main point, using examples, and appealing to both emotional and rational needs. Some people have gotten quite good at all of this. But as they've become more effective, they've also grown increasingly impatient with the limitations of face-to-face persuasion. They want to reach lots of people—all at once. They want to touch folks who won't come to a public meeting. If you sympathize with this desire, perhaps you'll be interested in the next chapter. It deals with the effectiveness of the mass media.

11

Mass Media

Last Sunday night I was interviewed on a radio program. Before the show I asked the producer what people typically listened to the program. He answered that the broadcast would be heard by people around the United States, South America, and Europe over a shortwave network. I was suddenly staggered by the thought that I had a chance to influence more people that night than I ever could face to face.

My appreciation of the persuasive potential of the mass media isn't limited to radio or TV. My grandfather founded two daily newspapers and my father carried on in the field of journalism. I was brought up with a healthy respect of the power of the press to change people's minds. I also appreciate the ability of a PA system to carry my voice to the edge of a crowd.

It seems that others are equally impressed with the possible impact of mass media. In the early 1970s American advertisers forked over 20 billion dollars a year for the opportunity of presenting their message through TV, radio, film, newspapers, magazines, signs, and billboards. By the time you read this, that figure will probably have doubled. Politicians also believe in the force of mass media to mold public opinion. The first act of dictators is to seize these means of communication. In fact, Marshall McLuhan claims that electronic media massage a person with messages to such an extent that they determine his attitudes and behavior.

Of course the obvious advantage of using the channels of mass communication is that they can multiply the number of hearings a message receives. The nineteenth century minister, Russell Conwell, spent his entire adult life traveling throughout the country delivering just one speech, "Acres of Diamonds." He gave this famous talk over 7000 times. Assuming a new audience of 1000 each night, Conwell could not have been heard by more than seven million people in his lifetime. Even on a bad night, network TV can deliver that many viewers for a single show.

Although the sheer numbers involved are awesome, they are not the entire story of media influence. Many people feel that mass media presentations have a persuasive power not shared by face to face communication. Luis Palau, "Latin America's Billy Graham," believes that he's more effective over TV than he is in his mass evangelism campaigns. Some ascribe almost magical qualities to the media. An announcer breathlessly states that this program is brought to you through the "modern miracle" of satellite TV. Broadcast critics claim that our children are being "brainwashed" by the media. Journalists assure us that "The pen is mightier than the sword," while public relations specialists modestly proclaim that they are "molders of public opinion." All of this suggests that the Christian persuader should jump with both feet into methods of mass communication. But before we are swept along by this media blitz, we need to ask some hard questions. Specifically:

1. Are the kinds of people we want to reach on the receiving end?
2. If they are, will they be likely to respond to our message?
3. What media strategies have the highest probability of success?

The answers to these questions need to come from solid research, not pious hopes or vague feelings. We often tend to shy away from such research—perhaps because we're afraid of what we'll find out. As you'll see in the next few pages, the evidence is not encouraging.

THE FLUSH FACTOR. Our search for the extent of media effectiveness begins at the municipal waterworks. About fifteen years ago, a

"Your royal command has been obeyed, Highness. Every town crier in the land is crying: 'Old King Cole is a merry ole soul.' Before nightfall we'll have them all believing it."

junior meter reader first noticed a strange fluctuation in water consumption. From 7-11 P.M. water demand was three times the normal rate exactly on the hour, and about double on the half-hour. Except for these few minutes, the pumping station delivered a steady flow. It didn't take a genius to figure out the reason. The majority of people across the city were watching TV during these prime time hours. They were enjoying their favorite shows—"I Love Lucy," "Bonanza," "Dr. Kildare," "The Dick Van Dyke Show," etc. They were watching to be entertained. When the advertisements came on between shows or during the half-hour station break, the people were no longer interested. They used the opportunity to go to the bathroom. The almost simultaneous use of a few thousand toilets accounted for the surge in water consumption. In the TV industry this phenomenon became known as the "flush factor," and it spelled trouble for those who claimed that the mass media could deliver an audience for any message.

It seems that media audiences are more selective than first imagined. The flush factor is only one example of a well-known theory in persuasion research, the *selective exposure hypothesis*. Briefly stated, the hypothesis predicts that people will voluntarily expose themselves to messages they already agree with or enjoy.[18] Conversely, they will systematically avoid presentations which they know will run counter to their views. The reasoning behind the prediction runs something like this: It's comforting to hear someone else presenting an idea that we already agree with. It reinforces our prejudices. We like to have others confirm our beliefs, and we'll often expose ourselves to this sort of thing. On the other hand, it's disturbing to read or hear a message that runs counter to our opinion. It's like hearing two discordant notes on the piano. We cringe and try to avoid such dissonance in the future.

There's a great deal of evidence which indicates that the selective exposure hypothesis is more than a hypothesis—that it is indeed what really happens. The most impressive study I know took place in Cincinnati after World War II.[19] It was concerned with citizen knowledge of the newly formed United Nations. The researchers conducted an initial survey to find out the amount of information the public had about the workings of the UN. They found that 45 percent of the people knew nothing about the UN—they didn't even recognize the name. Another 30 percent were slightly informed, while 25 percent fell into the category of "well-informed."

A foundation gave $500,000 for a six-month, saturation media campaign to raise the level of awareness. The money was used to buy advertising space in newspapers, broadcast spots on the radio, direct mailings, and billboard displays. In addition, speakers and discussion leaders were made available to churches, PTAs, and adult discussion groups. (A half million dollars could buy a lot of media exposure in the 1940s.) At the end of the campaign the researchers took another survey. They found that 45 percent of the people were still completely uninformed; 30 percent of the people were still moderately informed. There was a change, however. The 25 percent of the populace who were well-informed before the campaign were now *more* well-informed. In terms of attitude, these were the people who were already favorable toward the UN. They paid attention to the messages and therefore learned more. The other 75 percent merely ignored the messages. They turned the page, switched the dial, tossed the circular in the wastebasket, and didn't attend the meetings.

Selective exposure continues to be a fact of life today. In cities that offer competing daily newspapers, Republicans tend to buy the paper with the more conservative editorial policy, Democrats the liberal one. It is even more significant that most people choose to ignore the editorial page. Whereas the comics and "advice columns" such as Ann Landers or Abby VanBuren are read by over 80 percent of the subscribers, the editorial and opinion columns are read in less than 20 percent of the homes. This shows that people use the mass media primarily for entertainment, not as a whetstone for their ideas.

All of this has tremendous significance to the Christian advocate. Most religious communicators want to use the mass media to take their message to nonbelievers and to those who haven't heard the gospel; yet it seems that these are the people least likely to be on the receiving end. This discouraging fact was recently confirmed in a survey done by the Billy Graham Graduate School of Communications at Wheaton College. The main finding was that the audience for religious radio in the Chicago area is made up almost entirely of believers. We might label this "closed circuit" broadcasting. The term reflects the fact that the producers, financial supporters, and listeners of a religious broadcast are all like-minded believers.

The late Sam Shoemaker, an Episcopalian bishop, summed up the situation this way: "In the Great Commission the Lord has called us to be—like Peter—fishers of men. We've turned the commission around so that we have become merely keepers of the aquarium. Occasionally I take some fish out of your fishbowl and put them into mine, and you do the same with my bowl. But we're all tending the same fish."

Once the Christian broadcaster or journalist realizes that his audience consists mainly of those who already believe, he is in a position to make some intelligent decisions concerning the thrust of his message. It makes little sense to send evangelistic appeals to an audience which has already responded. Their needs are for Christian nurture, discussion of ethical problems, guidance on how best to spread the faith, instruction in biblical truth, and encouragement toward doing good works. We need to scratch where people itch. Responsible programming will meet these needs.

I have tried in this section to answer the question of whether or not the mass media can put us in touch with the type of person we're seeking to reach. Up to this point the answer has been No. Selective exposure means that those who receive our message are those who are already predisposed toward it. There are, however, notable exceptions in which the media have the ability to deliver a mass audience of people who ordinarily couldn't care less.

I've already suggested that people use the mass media primarily for entertainment. As long as there's sport, drama, comedy, or music available, the majority of the listening public will avoid teaching and preaching like the plague. They'll even dodge straight news. A few years ago one devious manager of a rock station played "Brahm's Lullaby" at five minutes to the hour—every hour of the day. His teen-age listeners found this music rather square and flipped to the other rock station on the dial. As the calculating manager had figured, the teenagers switched at precisely the time the competing station had their five-minute newscast. As a result, the kids quickly got the impression that the competing station had gone to an all news format, and they quit bothering to listen to it anymore. If there's no entertainment available, however, people will pay attention to public service, educational, and religious messages. To put it another way, there will always be spectators for the "only game in town."

One of the few times my children ever watched a Christian TV program was on a Palm Sunday morning in Niagara Falls, New York. I was trying to fly us back to our home in Chicago, but we were stuck in a dreary motel room due to lousy weather. My bored son and daughter checked out all three TV stations, but the only programs were two church services and a religious panel discussion about the meaning of

"You might as well knock it off, boys. Nielsen reports *nobody* is watching."

Good Friday. My kids chose the panel discussion as the lesser of the evils. But as the program continued, they became increasingly interested in the question of whether Jesus was just an unfortunate martyr, or if he had, in fact, planned ahead of time to sacrifice himself for mankind. This led into a great family discussion on the meaning of the Cross. For us, the Christian program had turned a dismal morning into an important time of insight and worship—but it wouldn't have happened if cartoons or anything else had been available. It happened because it was the only game in town.

I can think of only a few cases in the United States where Christian literature or broadcasts have a monopoly on the market. There are the occasional remote communities which can receive only religious broadcasts—station KCAM in central Alaska is a case in point. Some doctors' offices and hospital waiting rooms carry only religious literature. The Gideons place Bibles in otherwise barren motel rooms. But aside from these exceptions—and the Sunday type of saturation we experienced in Niagara Falls—the Christian can't expect to have the field to himself within the United States.

The situation is quite different in the emerging nations of the world. The Wycliffe Bible Translators work with some of the many unwritten tongues of the world. First, they develop an alphabet and grammar; second, they translate portions of Scripture into the new language; and third, they teach the people to read. They find that the newly literate person will eagerly devour anything in print that he can get his hands on. The mission radio station HCJB is the only Ecuadorian outlet to broadcast to the highland Quechua Indians in their own language. These people have been listening and responding in droves. This parallels my own childhood experience when American TV was in its infancy. The novelty of TV was so great that I'd dash home from school and plop down in front of the five-inch set—merely to watch a static test pattern. Not only did I watch, I responded. Hockey was the first sporting event televised in my home area and not surprisingly, it's one of my present-day passions.

One caution is in order for the broadcaster or publisher who has a monopoly. There's a danger in being the only game in town. It's very easy to get lazy and put out a sloppy product. Sooner or later competition enters the field and people realize how poorly they've been treated.

Another way of overcoming the effects of selective exposure is through entertainment itself. Since people use the mass media for relaxation and enjoyment, a message that's packaged as good entertainment will receive vast exposure. In short, "If you can't fight 'em, join 'em."

The obvious example in the educational field is "Sesame Street." Kids don't watch it to learn, they watch it for fun—but learn they do. In politics, the most effective practitioner I've heard is comedian Dick Gregory. People throng to his performances to laugh at his humor, and go away having sympathetically heard a social liberalism they'd reject in any other context.

Some Christian communicators have effectively used entertainment forms to get wide exposure for their message. Disc jockey Scott Ross employs popular rock and folk music as a springboard for brief commentaries on life. To tap into the Latin's passion for tear-jerking drama, Producciones Vozandes of Puerto Rico has videotaped a Christian soap opera for distribution on commercial TV in Central and South America. Crossroads of Canada's "Circle-Square" uses a "Sesame Street" format to introduce Christian truth to kids. Jim Johnson's *The Death of Kings* is a missionary aviation novel that has attracted a wide secular audience.

Notice that all of these examples have a certain restraint. They don't use music, humor, or drama as a "come on" and then blast the audience between the eyes with a bombastic sermon. The entertainment is always in the forefront with the message subtly woven into the background. Significantly, they aren't marketed through religious bookstores or on Christian stations. They are successful in overcoming selective exposure precisely because the audience doesn't anticipate a Christian message.

* * * *

Let's pause for a moment, because the whole notion of a "law" of selective exposure may really bother us. We need to consider the difference between the "laws" of physical science and the "laws" of human behavior. We're used to thinking about physical laws, such as gravity, in absolute terms. If someone steps off a cliff, we expect him to plummet downward—no exceptions. As Christians, we acknowledge that God can intervene and counteract this "law," but we've grown accustomed to the fact that he's made a cause-and-effect universe. That's why we call gravity a "law." It's also why we don't step off many cliffs.

The laws of human behavior seem much more tentative. One reason is that social science is a relatively new quest. Whereas Newton described the basics of gravitational force by 1700, organized study of human behavior is a post-World War II endeavor. We just don't know that much yet! Another complication arises from the delightful fact that humans have a certain element of choice. (See Chapter 3, "An Ethic for the Christian Persuader.") They can talk back. Just after we've summed up hundreds of protective actions into a basic "human drive for survival," some person thumbs his nose at our "law" and voluntarily steps off that aforementioned cliff. And perhaps most importantly, we must recognize that the Holy Spirit can step in and make the wisdom of men look foolish. As one psychologist friend of mine likes to put it, "God can stick in his finger and stir the pot."

Now this does not mean that human behavior is entirely random and unpredictable. I thank God that he has made us creatures of habit that will respond in a foreseeable pattern. Otherwise we would all go nuts with the uncertainty of how someone was going to react to us the next time. But it does suggest that laws of human behavior are dealing in the realm of the usual, the typical, the normal; in the majority of cases, etc. There can, and will be, exceptions.

Why bring up the issue of human predictability at this point in the chapter? Because this whole section has dealt with the "selective exposure hypothesis"—the prediction that people will consciously try to avoid hearing views opposed to their own. I've presented evidence that confirms the hypothesis and stated that non-Christians neither see nor listen to Christian mass media presentations. While this finding remains substantially true, we now see that there are exceptions. Whether because of conflicting needs, capricious choice, or the promptings of the Holy Spirit, some nonbelievers will be on the receiving end of Christian mass media. This raises the next major issue of the chapter: Will they respond favorably to our message?

KEEP THOSE CARDS AND LETTERS COMING IN. No student of mass communication can seriously doubt the media's impact upon society. Marshall McLuhan puts it this way: "We shape our tools, and they in turn shape us."[20] For example, man invented the printing press, but this invention then molded man's way of thinking. Printing is sequential. Word follows word, page follows page. The printing press taught man to think in an ordered sequence. The invention of the radio and TV, however, changed this. The electronic media catapulted us into an age of "all at onceness," in which we're bombarded simultaneously by a thousand different happenings. As a result of electronic communication, we now live in a global village where last night's revolution in Africa is this morning's breakfast conversation in America. Detached cognitive thought is out; immediate emotional reaction is in.

We no longer check another's response by saying, "Do you follow me?" but rather ask, "How does that grab you?"

Whether or not we buy McLuhan's analysis, we must admit that the media have a profound influence on current events. The President's Commission on Civil Disorder cited TV as a major factor in the "long hot summer" of riots in 1963. TV exposed ghetto-dwellers to a quality of life that they had never imagined possible. This helped build the frustration which broke out into violence in the Watts district of Los Angeles. Films of the looting and burning in the streets triggered similar outbreaks in major U.S. cities throughout the summer.

The media also affect how we interpret current events. We judge how important something is by whether or not it makes the 6:00 P.M. network news. A man attains political fame when he gets his picture on the front of *TIME* magazine. In the pop entertainment world, the cover of *Rolling Stone* has equal stature. Because of the media, Viet Nam had a different meaning to us than Korea or other unpopular wars. For the first time, American civilians could actually see war atrocities as they happened—in living color. Anti-war protests were fueled by scenes of men shot right in our own living room.

We can see that the media do influence attitudes and alter behavior. Print and broadcast outlets are agents of change. But the changes they produce often appear to be unintended by-products of watching TV or reading a paper. How about audience reaction to the direct appeal of an ad, editorial, public service message, or sermon? Will a reasonable percentage of people who are exposed to a mass media appeal respond favorably? This is information the Christian persuader desperately needs if he's going to buy time on the air or space in the press. Unfortunately, research in this area is somewhat sketchy, and the answers that we do have are not encouraging. It's not without reason that the radio minister concludes his program with the plaintive request, "Keep those cards and letters coming in."

One way of gauging audience reaction is to make a direct media appeal for a behavioral response, and then tot up the results. This was done during World War II when singer Kate Smith went on nationwide radio to persuade people to buy war bonds.[21] Now unless you're over forty or a regular fan of the Philadelphia Flyer hockey games, you may not appreciate Kate Smith's fame. During the 1940s, she was the country's most popular female singer. There wasn't a dry eye in the house when Kate sang "God Bless America." The bond drive was a novel event in that she vowed to broadcast for eighteen straight hours in an effort to achieve the dollar goal of the campaign. Radio-a-thons and TV marathons are old hat today, but this was the first of its kind back then. It caught the imagination of the country. Almost all adults listened to the broadcast sometime during the program. People would meet in the street and anxiously ask, "Do you think Kate can hold out?" There was tremendous listener appreciation of Miss Smith's physical sacrifice as her voice began to crack, and there was an equal approval around the nation of her patriotic aim—raising money for the war effort. In short, the conditions were ideal for a favorable audience response to a mass media appeal.

What happened? Telephone pledges rolled in from around the country. Thousands and thousands of people bought bonds either during or immediately following the broadcast. Millions of dollars were raised through the effort. Advertising agencies and public relations firms heralded the results as dramatic evidence of the mass media's persuasive impact. It was only later that a dispassionate analysis revealed what little influence the whole spectacular had upon audience behavior.

The first thing the postmortem revealed was that less than one percent of the listeners actually bought a victory bond. This dispelled the myth that the media automatically mobilize those on the receiving end into united action. People still acted as individuals, and given the size of the audience, very few of them responded with an actual purchase. It was then discovered that almost all the folks who bought bonds were already regular purchasers. With few exceptions, Kate Smith's appeal was unable to tap the vast pool of non-bond buyers. This was a blow to the idea that the media have the power to convert people from one side to the other.

The final piece of discouraging news came later. The researchers found out that while there was a surge in bond subscription immediately after the radio-a-thon, there was also a corresponding slump in sales the following months. Apparently those who responded to Miss Smith's persuasion merely accelerated their buying. They bought an extra bond or two that month, but made up for it by skipping the next time they would normally buy. The net long-term increase in defense dollars for the country was practically zero.

Thirty years later, response to mass media persuasion is still minimal. The 1975 Super Bowl broadcast delivered a nationwide audience of 60 million people. The *Miami Herald* ran a survey to see whether or not city viewers could identify the sponsors following the telecast.[22] They figured—and rightly so—that sponsor awareness is a first condition of ad effectiveness. If people can't even recall the name of the product, they aren't likely to go out and buy it. The response varied with the product. Colt 45 Malt Liquor and Equitable Life Insurance were forgotten by 99 percent of those surveyed. Datsun and Master Lock did better—3 percent of the viewers remembered their ad. Chrysler's ads had the highest recall, but only 25 percent of the people could identify them as a sponsor even though they had four separate messages.

Are the executives of America's large corporations stupid? Why spend millions of dollars a year on advertising when only a small percentage of the media audience will be influenced? The answer lies not in stupidity but in the sheer size of the market. If a commercial advertiser can affect the buying behavior of just 1 percent of his audience, his gross sales will increase by millions of dollars. This happened with Marlboro cigarettes. Twenty-five years ago, Marlboro had an image as a rich society lady's cigarette. A massive media campaign redefined the Marlboro smoker as a rugged outdoorsman—a no-nonsense westerner with a tattoo on the back of his hand. In a period of one year, Marlboro jumped from less than 1 percent of tobacco sales to over 4 percent. This may not seem like much in absolute terms, but the effect on the P & L statement was fantastic.

Now we need to note that Marlboro had three advantages not shared by us as Christian communicators. In the first place, they had lots of money to spend on the media campaign. They were able to buy time for repeated nationwide exposures. These kind of funds just aren't available to nonprofit organizations, Christian or otherwise. Second, they were asking for minimal behavior change. They weren't attempting to get people to stop smoking, a deeply ego-involving act that's highly resistant to change. They were merely asking smokers to change brands. The Christian persuader's aim, on the other hand, is a whopping lifestyle change in areas that are central to people. Finally, Marlboro didn't have to worry if some folks were turned off by their ads. The important issue was increased sales. If some nonsmokers snickered at the messages—well, that was just too bad. Those people weren't going to buy anyway. This kind of thinking is a luxury Christians can't afford. Our Lord has shown us that we must be concerned for all men. It's not furthering the kingdom of God if we drive ten people away for every one we attract.

Where have we come so far in this section? I've suggested that although the media have a tremendous sociological impact, they receive only a small response when used for direct persuasive appeals. This fact has been well-known to media strategists for years. Some have put forth a theory of indirect media influence called the "two-step flow of communication."[23] These theorists suggest that the media affect a relatively small, but influential, segment of society. Those affected tend to be opinion leaders among their own circle of friends. Through face-to-face communication they spread the word which was received through radio, TV, or the press. Thus the first step is one of media influence upon the few, and the second step is interpersonal persuasion of the many.

The two-step flow is a rather clever idea, and for many years it held sway in the field of communication. Its only drawback is that it's not supported by the facts. The mass media actually do a pretty good job of spreading information—not just to a few opinion leaders, but to the average man in the street as well. But making people aware of a new idea is not the same thing as getting them to accept it. It's at this point that interpersonal communication has the advantage. These facts have led to a modern modification of the two-step flow: 1) Mass media spreads the word; 2) Face-to-face communication makes it believable.

The whole Watergate mess is a case in point. Month after month the news media presented startling evidence about corruption in government without noticeable results. The public was aware of the accusations, it just didn't believe them. For most people, it took the word of a friend or the testimony of someone they respected to validate the charges.

I've known this to happen in radio evangelism. For years a missionary group broadcast the gospel into the jungles of Costa Rica. The Indians listened to the message and seemed to understand the meaning, but none of them yielded to it. Occasionally a few men would migrate to San Jose in search of a good job. While in the city, one of these men fell into a group of Christians and professed faith in Jesus Christ. A revival swept through his tribe about two months after he returned to the village. For the first time, the people had a visible model to legitimatize the word they heard over the radio—and they responded en masse.

I think this updated version of the two-step flow presents a realistic picture of the persuasive force of mass communications. In and of themselves, the media have little power to influence. Or to put it in technical terms, mass communication does not ordinarily serve as a necessary and sufficient cause of audience effects. This is bad news for the Christian advocate who plans to use printed or broadcast messages as the sole means of reaching people with the faith. We saw in the first section that the people he wants most in his audience are the ones least likely to be there. We now see in addition that those who *are* on the receiving end probably won't accept the message without having lots of confirmation from those around them.

In the face of all this, what should the Christian do? Shall we skip the means of mass communication because of their relatively low impact? No! It's possible to use media channels selectively in order to influence men to choose for God. The final section of this chapter suggests how.

STRIKING A RESPONSIVE CHORD. The 1964 presidential election pitted Senator Barry Goldwater against incumbent Lyndon Johnson. A Johnson media man created a simple one-shot television spot which literally demolished Goldwater's chances. The spot appeared during the popular "Monday Night at the Movies." It created such a furor of controversy that it was never shown again, but its devastating impact upon millions of viewers remained. What was the thrust of the commercial, and why was it so effective? Its creator, Tony Schwartz, describes it in these terms:

The spot shows a little girl in a field counting petals on a daisy. As her count reaches ten, the visual motion is frozen and the viewer hears a countdown. When the countdown reaches zero, we see a nuclear explosion and hear President Johnson say, "These are the stakes, to make a world in which all God's children can live, or to go into the darkness.

*Either we must love each other or we must die.'' As the screen goes
black at the end, white lettering appears stating, "On November 3rd,
Vote for President Johnson.''*

*Nowhere in the spot is Goldwater mentioned. There is not even an
indirect reference to Goldwater. Indeed, someone unfamiliar with the
political climate in 1964 and viewing the spot today will not perceive
any allusion at all to Goldwater. Then why did it bring such a reaction
in 1964? Well, Senator Goldwater had stated previously that he supported the use of tactical atomic weapons. The commercial evoked a
deep feeling in many people that Goldwater might actually use nuclear
weapons. This mistrust was not in the Daisy spot. It was in the people
who viewed the commercial. The stimuli of the film and sound evoked
these feelings and allowed people to express what they inherently
believed.*[24]

Schwartz claims the ad was effective because it struck a responsive
chord. It didn't try to interject new material, it merely called to the
surface a deeply felt emotion which lay dormant among the audience. I
think he's right. The typical Christian writer or broadcaster strives
against his stubborn audience, trying to get them to accept *his* words.
The resultant sounds of books closing and dials turning can be heard
throughout the world. We're much better off when we tap into a person's past experiences and associations. This stimulates him to self-
generate the idea we want him to consider.

It's kind of like playing charades. You go through lots of motion in
an effort to get me to create the words you have in mind. You can't
transfer them. You must get me to call them up for myself. And just as
charades is a nonverbal game, the process of eliciting response is best
accomplished through nonverbal cues. The smell of leaves burning
makes me remember fall football games. The melody of "September
Song" calls to mind a gal I dated in high school. The sight of an
airplane excites a feeling of freedom within me, and the touch of something sharp stirs up old fears of being cut with a knife. Notice that all of
these emotional reactions come out of my past, and each is triggered by
some nonverbal association. These responses, and many more, are
available to the media communicator. He can get me to persuade myself
if he strikes a responsive chord. Let me give you an example.

I am against adultery. (I hope that doesn't come as a surprise to my readers.) I strongly believe in sexual fidelity and am firmly committed to the position that intercourse outside marriage violates the law of God. At the same time I must be honest and recognize that there are unpure sexual desires within me. I take the sinfulness of man quite seriously, because I can see it in myself. Now I have no problem when I'm confronted with a blatant appeal for free love, a so-called "open marriage" or any other form of unfaithfulness. I can easily dismiss these as running counter to my attitude. When I saw the movie *Doctor Zhivago*, however, I found myself mentally applauding the fact that Omar Sharif was about to abandon his wife and jump into the arms of Julie Christie. What prompted this reaction in me?

In the first place, I went to the movie for entertainment, not to hear a message. This meant that I wasn't prepared to resist a persuasive appeal. I quickly came to identify with Zhivago—his dreams for achievement, his anguish in the Russian revolution, and his attraction to the army nurse, Lara, during their nightmarish months on the battlefield. Although I'm not a doctor, have never lived through a revolution, nor been in the army, I could put myself in his shoes. I too have had dreams, frustrations, and feelings of desire. These emotions flooded into consciousness as the images on the screen reminded me of past experiences. For a few hours I became Zhivago. I also associated the flowing music and stunning photography with other things in life that are beautiful and pure. My responses signaled me that what I was seeing in the movie was OK. The film had found in me a responsive chord.

I'm not unique. All humans have a conflicting variety of past experiences, associations, and desires. Effective media persuasion is a matter of stimulating a tendency that's already there. Some of man's reactions are noble and good. Others are selfish and base. The job of the Christian persuader is to identify those responses in a particular audience which warm them toward God. He can then concentrate on fanning those embers.

There are a number of ways a Christian communicator can increase his chances of "resonating" with an audience. The Zhivago example demonstrates the tremendous power of drama to elicit a response. Any well-conceived narrative will create a second-hand reality for the reader/listener. Once he's drawn into the images of a new world, he'll react to the events in the story as if they're really happening to him. (For a fuller account of the persuasive impact of imagery, see Chapter 7, "Role Play.")

A few weeks before I became a Christian, I read Lloyd Douglas' novel *The Robe*. The book is a fictionalized account of the Roman centurion who crucified Jesus. The legionnaire gambles at the foot of the Cross for Christ's robe. After he wins, he finds its touch repugnant and orders his slave to throw it away. In the following years he's tortured by guilt and fear. He finds peace only when he locates the robe and subsequently tosses in his lot with the Christians. Now it's true that there's nothing particularly scriptural about this story. But it did more to attract me to the power of Jesus Christ than all the sermons I'd ever heard.

Unfortunately most Christian fiction is blatantly transparent. The villain is the kind of person who stomps on baby chicks, and the heroine wins the "Shirley Temple Miss-Goody-Two-Shoes" award for being unbelievably pure. And that's the problem. This kind of morality play fails to create a second-hand reality because the characters aren't believable. The reader or listener simply can't identify with them. There's a great need for more Christian authors and playwrights who will people their works *not* with devils and angels, but with human beings who sweat and occasionally have to go to the bathroom.

Another way the media user can insure striking a responsive chord is to aim at one specific type of audience. We often try to be all things to all men and end up appealing to no one. A missionary radio broadcaster recently complained to me concerning the narrowness of his audience. "Our research shows that over half the people that listen to our show are male shortwave radio hams between the ages of fifteen to twenty-five," he moaned. As I see it, the sameness of his audience isn't a problem, it's an asset. He can spend lots of time around radio hams to find out what makes them tick, and then program to meet their exact felt needs. The idea of targeting a message for a specific type of audience has many labels. In broadcasting, it's called "market segmentation." In journalism, it's referred to as "subscriber profile analysis." In the field of public address, the phrase is "audience adaptation." Whatever we call it, we need to do it!

The term mass media is a bit deceptive. It gives the impression that we can reach a *variety* of people at the same time. We can't! But it is possible to reach a number of *similar* people at the same time. The key is to zero in on their unique needs. I'd much rather try to reach a group of left-handed bus drivers who bowl on Tuesday nights than an audience of dissimilar people. And if I create my appeal with the bus driver group in mind, they'll be the ones on the receiving end.

There's a general theory of persuasion called "attribution theory." It seeks to explain how we come to hold our beliefs about ourselves and the world around us. One part of the theory is especially applicable to mass communication. This is the prediction that people will attribute greater validity to ideas which come to them 1) across sources, 2) across time, and 3) across channels. If I hear the same idea from Walter Cronkite, Howard Cosell, the principal of my son's school, and my brother-in-law, I'll tend to believe it more than if just one of them says it. In like manner, it'll seem more credible if I'm exposed to it repeatedly over a two-year period than if I get it through a one-shot presentation. And finally, the message will have greater impact if it comes on TV, radio, billboards, in flyers, newspapers, books, magazines, movies, public speeches, and over-the-fence conversations. Attribution theory therefore recommends that Christians not put all their eggs in one communication basket. We need to develop an effective media mix which employs multiple modes of communication. This does not just mean taking an effective sermon and broadcasting it verbatim over radio or printing its text in a magazine. Each form of mass communication is distinct and we need to tailor-make our presentation to its specific requirements.

* * * *

A few weeks ago my children and I were working alone in the fellowship hall of our church. The kids lost interest in the task when they discovered a working PA system. They had a tremendous sense of power as they sang, told jokes, and pretended to broadcast sporting events into the microphone. But they soon tired of their play as they realized it's not enough to have the mechanical means to blat out the sound of your voice. You have to say something worth hearing and have someone willing to listen to it.

And so it is with the Christian's use of mass communication. The media are only tools. They aren't the end-all and be-all of Christian witness, nor the ultimate solution to the Great Commission. But they have been given to us by God to be used selectively and creatively in gaining a response to his love.

MAKE HARD

12

How to Prevent Belief

You may find the title of this chapter a bit curious. This is a book about persuasion. Almost all of the material in it is designed to help the individual Christian promote change in other people's beliefs, feelings, and actions toward Jesus Christ. Why spend time considering ways in which interpersonal influence can be minimized or thwarted?

The first reason has already been presented in the opening chapter. I suggested that persuasion is a three-step process. Previous attitudes must first be melted or thawed before the second step of molding or change takes place. But this is not enough. The new attitudes need to be firmed up so that they become resistant to later outside influences. In other words, we try to prevent further change in belief. Once a person believes in Jesus Christ, we want to make sure he doesn't revert back to old beliefs or subscribe to new unbiblical doctrines.

And when a person has escaped from the wicked ways of the world by learning about our Lord and Savior Jesus Christ, and then gets tangled up with sin and becomes its slave again, he is worse off than he was before (2 Peter 2:20, TLB).

There's another reason to know how to induce resistance to persuasion. As proclaimers of the gospel, we need to be careful that we don't do it! It's possible that some of our attempts to draw people into the body of Christ might inadvertently freeze them into their present non-Christian position. If we understand the mechanism that causes resistance, we won't fall into that trap.

A VACCINE FOR HERESY. We're all familiar with the medical practice of vaccination. It's a doctor's way of making us resistant to a disease we've never had. He can spare us the dangers of polio, smallpox, measles, and mumps through the process of immunization. It's also possible to inoculate people against new *beliefs*. The vaccination process is really quite similar. We'll take a look at this medical analogy in order to understand how to prevent persuasion.

Next year my whole family is going to Ecuador where I will teach a course in Quito. The U. S. State Department suggests that all of us get smallpox vaccinations before we go. The reason for this precaution is simple. Smallpox is almost unknown in the United States. None of us have ever been exposed to the disease, so our systems have never prepared antibodies to fight the smallpox virus. If we were exposed to smallpox out of the country, we'd be quite susceptible to the attack.

This is true with some of our beliefs. They've developed in a "germfree" environment, without question or attack. Such a "hothouse" belief is vulnerable for two reasons. First of all, we may not even realize that there's another way of thinking. When suddenly confronted by a winsome presentation of a new idea, we can easily be swept away by its novelty. Secondly, even if we know there are opposing opinions, we've never practiced defending against them. We haven't built up an immunity to views which run counter to our original attitudes.

It's easy to see how this can happen with belief in God. Let's suppose a child is raised in a Christian home; he's surrounded by parents and relatives who love the Lord. His parents send him to a Christian school so that he will not be contaminated by the world, and in the summer he goes to a Christian camp. Most of his non-school social activities are centered in the church. In short, he has been immersed in a supportive environment which is congenial to his Christian faith. Although his faith in God may appear quite strong, in actuality it is very susceptible to change when he's exposed to a virile attack from the other side. This

"One of these days we ought to tell him he was adopted."

often happens when he goes to college or gets a job. It's one of the reasons why many fellows and gals lose their faith when they first leave home.

The reverse can also be true. A person who is raised in a completely agnostic environment may be overwhelmed when he meets a loving Christian who speaks intimately about Jesus Christ. Whatever a person's initial attitude, it is vulnerable to radical change if it has been nurtured in a germfree atmosphere.

Let's return to the smallpox analogy. When my family goes for a vaccination, the doctor will scratch a small drop of toxin into the skin. Make no mistake—he's not giving us medicine to help fight smallpox. He's actually placing a small dose of the virus into our bloodstream so that we will contract a mild case of the disease. This will be hard for my children to understand when their left arm breaks out in a puffy, itching, red rash. It won't make sense to them that the doctor wants them to get slightly sick in order to prevent greater illness later. What they don't comprehend is that as our body is exposed to a manageable amount of germs, it builds up antibodies which keep us from getting the whole disease later.

The same is true in the area of beliefs. If we want to help prevent a major shift of attitude away from Christian truth, we need to inoculate a person against falsehood. Pretending it doesn't exist is a mistake. Right now my son believes in the bodily resurrection of Jesus Christ. To him, it's silly to think otherwise. But I need to warn him that many people don't believe in the resurrection, and he should know some of their arguments. In this way he'll be motivated to ward off their attack, and at the same time he'll have some practice in resisting their persuasion. William McGuire, the founder of inoculation theory, calls this a "vaccine for brainwash."

The theory of belief inoculation suggests that it is easier to prevent a person from losing his initial faith than it is to restore that belief once it has been lost. In other words, an ounce of prevention is worth a pound of cure. McGuire's research has shown the validity of that saying. I'm going to present the various twists and turns of McGuire's work because it's like a good mystery story—the skilled investigator tracking clues wherever they lead.[25]

TESTING IT IN THE LAB. In order to test the effect of belief inoculation, McGuire had to first find a non-controversial position on which all would agree, not even considering the possibility of an opposing viewpoint. Toothbrushing turned out to be one such area. Everyone he questioned thought that it was a fine thing to brush their teeth after every meal. Apparently the American Dental Association has been eminently successful in implanting that idea into our minds. (Note that this agreement doesn't mean we actually *do* brush after every meal, just that we *believe* it's a good idea. McGuire's work is in the area of beliefs, not behavior.)

McGuire then prepared a persuasive message which advocated the unthinkable—namely that brushing is bad for the teeth. Among other things, the message suggested that brushing scrapes off the protective enamel and dilutes the natural cleansing agent in saliva.

As the first part of his six-stage study, McGuire simply presented his anti-toothbrushing message to a number of different audiences. This would be similar to my never discussing the fact that many people don't believe in the resurrection, and then letting my son hear their doubts from them. Just as McGuire had predicted, people were easily swayed to this new point of view. He had established that beliefs nurtured in a protected environment are quite susceptible to change.

Before trying various forms of inoculation, he decided to test the traditional way of preparing people to maintain their beliefs—reinforcing their already held attitudes. He provided folks with vast amounts of information supporting the practice of frequent toothbrushing. In other words, he gave a boost to the concept in which they already believed. A parallel situation would be for me to present my son with five or six reasons for believing in the resurrection, without pointing out that many believe otherwise, or what their reasons are.

Initially it looked as if this strategy was highly successful. Those who heard the concept boost voiced opinions which were militantly in favor of frequent brushing. These results were temporary, however. As soon as they heard the message which attacked toothbrushing, they abandoned their original belief. In fact, this group of people ended up more anti-toothbrushing than the group which had no concept boost! McGuire calls this the "paper tiger" effect. When original beliefs are reinforced, it looks like the person can fight off any attack of his beliefs. But when the attack comes, his beliefs collapse.

Suppose I merely warn Jim that he'll run across many people who think the resurrection is like the existence of Santa Claus, a fable or myth. I don't deal with the arguments pro or con, but only caution him that he'll hear persuasive appeals on the other side. McGuire tried this type of warning in the third stage of his investigation. He found that it had a beneficial effect on preventing a change in belief. People were still swayed by the anti-brushing message, but knowing that an attack was coming tempered its effect by making listeners more resistant to the attempt.

At this point McGuire tested the vaccination technique. He not only warned people that an attack was coming, he gave them a small dose of the arguments they would later hear. There was not so much material that they would be convinced toothbrushing was bad, but there was enough to bother them—to get them questioning and counterarguing. The results were encouraging. The inoculation prevented a radical change of belief. When people heard the actual persuasive attack, they were only moderately swayed—much less than when they received only the warning.

The researcher noted a problem, however. He had found that inoculating people with a small dose of the opposing viewpoint would stimulate them to prepare a defense. But he also discovered they weren't very good at it. They were so unpracticed at defending previously unchallenged beliefs that they really didn't know where to begin. He wondered if it wouldn't help to provide them with a refutation of the other side. This would be like first vaccinating someone with smallpox toxin and then giving him a shot of penicillin to help fight the germs. He tried it and found this more effective than belief vaccination alone. In

"Either you have the wrong number or the student you're calling hasn't taken over my office yet."

fact, there was little attitude change at all when the experimental participants heard the anti-toothbrushing message.

Was there any way to prevent even this small shift in belief? McGuire thought there might be. He speculated that the problem with giving the complete refutation of opposing arguments is that people then don't do any cognitive work themselves. By spoon-feeding all of the answers, we rob a man of the opportunity to do the mental calisthenics which strengthen his ability to defend against any attack. On the other hand, he'd already discovered that it was less effective to inoculate without giving any help in refuting the opposition. He ultimately came to the conclusion that it was best to inoculate and then give a *partial* refutation. This had the best of both worlds going for it. The person wouldn't be discouraged. He'd see that it was possible to answer deviant views and he'd get some help on how to do it. Yet he would still have to do some of the refutation on his own.

In the sixth and final stage of his research, McGuire tried this technique of vaccination plus partial refutation. He found that it raised resistance to such a high level that people didn't catch the disease. They never lost their faith in toothbrushing!

PUTTING IT INTO PRACTICE. The chart below summarizes McGuire's work. As you can again see, the *least* effective way of inducing resistance to persuasion is by constantly reinforcing what a person already believes without ever telling him there's another side. Unfortunately this is what we often do in Christian circles. If a person is raised in a Christian environment, we tend to shield him from considering worldly ideas that run counter to the gospel. If, on the other hand, he's a recent convert, we often encourage him to believe that from now on every day with Jesus will be sweeter than the day before. Both approaches render the Christian incapable of handling later doubts. When reality crashes in, his Christian convictions are easily shaken or toppled.

The chart also reminds us that the most effective way of preventing persuasion is by showing the other side to a person and then helping him to deal with it. Jesus did this for his disciples. He warned them of the leaven of the Pharisees, explained how others would deny his Lordship, and cautioned them about events that would tend to shake their faith after he left the earth. In short, he inoculated them.

SUMMARY OF MCGUIRE'S WORK
*Amount of Opinion Change
when Traditional Belief Is Challenged*

No Preparation	****************************
Concept Boost of Previous Belief	*********************************
Warning of Future Attack	**********************
Inoculation	**********
Inoculation plus Refutation	******
Inoculation plus Partial Refutation	**

But he didn't stop there. He showed them how to refute wrong belief by his teachings and example. Finally, he let the disciples do some of the work themselves, sending them out into the countryside two by two.

I recently observed a Young Life camp which effectively applied the inoculation approach to Christian high school seniors who were preparing to go to college. Most of the fellows and gals were relatively new Christians, and their childlike faith might easily be shaken on a secular university campus. The College Prep week was designed to prepare them to hold onto their beliefs when in a hostile environment. Lectures on non-Christian world views, meetings with Christian college students, and discussions with fellow graduates about anticipated problems all served as a small dose of vaccine.

Perhaps the most effective technique the camp employed was having counselors role play different types of people the students were likely to meet the following year. One counselor wore a sign that said "Atheist" for the entire week. He would talk with individual campers at meals and around the grounds trying to get them to adopt this point of view. If the student had difficulty defending the Christian position, the counselor would step out of his role and help him to see the inconsistent assumptions of the atheistic position. Other staff enacted different roles—Scientific Determinist, Communist, Playboy, Humanist, Skeptic, Buddhist, and Mormon. In this way students were made aware of opposing points of view and had practice dealing with them without getting in over their heads. They became well-prepared to be the Christian salt of the campus without losing their savor.

TURNING THEM OFF. At the start of this chapter I suggested that it would be tragic if somehow we inoculated others against the Christian faith. This is not as farfetched as it might seem. In his clever satire *The Gospel Blimp*, Joe Bayly pictures the ardent Christian who wants to evangelize his town. He decides to purchase a blimp to fly over the city towing a banner and dropping tracts. He assumes that God's Word will not return void, believing that it's impossible for any proclamation of the gospel to have a harmful effect. His neighbors, however, get a very partial dose—and not a very attractive one—of the Christian message. They mentally counterargue and thus build up resistance to religious persuasion later on.

I've seen a similar phenomenon occur in Wheaton, Illinois. In many ways Wheaton is the evangelical center of America. It is the home of my school, Wheaton College. Some fifty-seven different Christian organizations have their headquarters within its boundaries. There are, in fact, whole blocks of homes in the community without a non-Christian family. The result is that most people in town have been "witnessed to." Every barber has been evangelized. Because many townspeople have successfully resisted small doses of the gospel, they have become inoculated against further consideration of the faith.

Inoculation occurs whenever we try to mold someone's opinion without melting them first—making certain that they are at least open to our influence. The high-pressure soul-winner who accosts all the people he meets on a plane or bus does so believing that this may be the only time in their lives that they will consider Jesus. Unfortunately, because of inoculation, he may be right. His very act induces a resistance to Christian persuasion in many people. This renders them immune to a more comprehensive and sympathetic presentation of the gospel later on.

I've always been impressed by the candor of D. L. Moody's comment when he was criticized for his persuasive tactics. He answered, "You don't think much of my methods. I don't either. But I like my way of doing it better than your way of not doing it." Because of inoculation effects, however, some methods of evangelization are worse in the long run than no attempt at all.

The implication of inoculation theory is that Christian persuasion should not be a "hit and run" affair. If we care enough about a person to share our Lord with him, we need to make sure that he apprehends the whole range of the justice and love of Jesus Christ. This may take time, energy, and commitment. But if it's not worth the effort, we have no business messing up another Christian's chance to point effectively to the Savior.

13

Behavior

Before I was born, a man named La Piere sent out letters to the managers of 256 hotels and restaurants across the southern half of the United States.[26] He told them that he was planning to tour the south with two Chinese companions and he wanted to know ahead of time whether they would be served. Ninety-two percent of the businesses replied that they did *not* serve Chinese and that La Piere could save himself considerable embarrassment by not showing up with such undesirables. He wasn't surprised. Racial prejudice was a part of southern life in the 1930s, and this was long before a ban was placed on discrimination in interstate commerce. La Piere ignored the managers' advice, however. Accompanied by a Chinese man and his wife, he visited every one of the establishments that said they'd refuse service. Surprise! Ninety-nine percent of the places admitted the oriental couple, and almost all did so without a hassle.

There are many possible explanations for the discrepancy between what they claimed they'd do and what they actually did. Perhaps they pictured two sweaty coolies ready to start a tong war, whereas the couple who showed up were quite pleasant and neatly dressed. Maybe the managers were afraid that kicking them out would cause a public disturbance. Then again it might just be that it's much harder to tell someone face-to-face that you don't want them than it is to reject them through an impersonal letter. Or it's possible that in some cases an employee other than the manager was the one who seated or registered the couple. Whatever the reason, La Piere's study points up something that's a consistent finding in the field of persuasion—that a person may *say* he feels one thing, and then turn right around and *do* something completely different.

That's why this chapter. Since a man's behavior doesn't always follow in step with his attitude, we need to take a concentrated look at ways of affecting another's action. I'm going to suggest six specific approaches to alter behavior. One is the traditional route—the others work. I've selected two problem areas as a means of illustrating how these methods might be used by the persuasive Christian. The first has to do with witness, the second with sex.

I don't need to elaborate on the importance of encouraging other Christians to verbally share their faith with nonbelievers. If you've gotten this far in the book, you're probably committed to that task. I realize that by choosing sex as my second example, I may turn off some of my readers. But I'm willing to take that risk because the whole area of physical relationships is a battleground for many Christians. I know that as a young Christian, this was the focus of my biggest struggles in moral conduct. By the grace of God I didn't enter the growing ranks of those experiencing premarital sex, but I lost some battles along the way. The problem isn't limited to adolescence. Counselors say that extramarital sex among believers is a fact of life. Some things haven't changed much since Corinth. So what I'm going to do is describe six methods of behavior change. After each explanation, I'll show how the technique can be used in the service of promoting the faith and cooling an over-warm physical relationship.

IS THE HAND BONE CONNECTED TO THE HEAD BONE?
The way we usually try to get people to change what they do is by attempting to shift their whole attitude. This traditional approach assumes that behavior follows attitude. If a man is really sold on something, he'll act on it.

I've already indicated that this way doesn't always work. Part of the problem is that a single act is spawned by a whole host of attitudes.

Take a look at what a huge task it is to stimulate people to speak of their faith by going this route. A partial list of the attitudes involved includes love for God, love for fellowman, the truth of the gospel, feeling that others are lost without it, and our opinion of ourselves as ambassadors of Christ. The job is equally awesome when using attitudes to affect behavior in sexual relations. Views of the opposite sex, the relative importance of touch, our understanding of marriage, and perception of our bodies as temples of the Holy Spirit are just a few of the relevant opinion areas. Even if we're successful in affecting all of these attitudes, the other person may miss the connection between them and what he does.

There's another problem with assuming that outward behavior will be consistent with inward conviction. It ignores the element of behavioral cost.[27] I may really believe that it's important to give the world an account of the hope that's in me, but I may also be scared stiff to broach topics of personal belief. You can preach about my obligation to share my faith till you're blue in the face, and I'll agree with you right down the line. But my emotional fear of rejection will render me mute. When we expect attitude change to produce behavior change, we neglect the fact that switching our actions may have a tremendous psychological cost. There's a separate cost attached to every possible action. It's as if we have a series of hurdles stretched out before us. Our love for the Lord and other people may be strong enough to get us over some of the hurdles. But we'll trip over the biggies every time. A small change in attitude isn't going to help us clear a towering obstacle created by a fear of rejection.

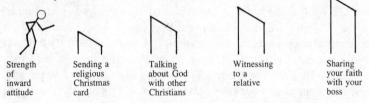

Strength of inward attitude   Sending a religious Christmas card   Talking about God with other Christians   Witnessing to a relative   Sharing your faith with your boss

So behavior doesn't always follow attitudes. As a matter of fact, more often than not it seems to work the other way around. Attitudes follow behavior. If you can get a person to do something voluntarily, he'll usually adjust his thinking to be consistent with his action. A man who's sexually faithful to his wife will come to hold strong convictions about marital fidelity. If he starts cheating on her, however, he'll come up with all sorts of rationalizations to justify his behavior. So the traditional approach to changing actions is inadequate. There are other methods which offer promise of success. We'll take a look at these next.

ENVIRONMENTAL ENGINEERING. For years the National Safety Council spent thousands of dollars trying to persuade people to fasten their auto seat belts. The programs were a flop. Then they switched their efforts and got Congress to pass a law requiring that a buzzer sound when the straps weren't buckled. The buzzer is so irritating that people use the belts to get rid of the sound. This is an example of a situational approach to behavior change. The method is based on the idea that people act in response to their environment. If you want to change a person, change the situation that surrounds him. Note that this was the basic assumption of shaping procedure presented in Chapter 11. Alter the situation to maximize the benefits and to minimize the costs of a given action, and both the pigeon and the person will change.

How would this work with a person who'd gotten in too deep in a physical relationship? It would mean recognizing that some situations are too hot to handle no matter how good his intentions. No way is he going to keep his hands off the girl if they're alone in a parked car on a country lane on a warm June night. I once had a college coed come to me in tears because she'd slept with a guy the week before. Believe it or not, she accepted the fellow's invitation to spend the night in a motel but told me that she hadn't planned on making love. I was incredulous! Some circumstances are so clear-cut that your behavior is a foregone conclusion once you enter the situation. If a couple is honestly trying to avoid too much physical intimacy, there are some specific steps they can take. They'd be well advised to avoid hanging around solely with another couple that's outwardly affectionate, not to take too much time praying together (just the two of them), and in general to spend the majority of their time around lots of other people. Circumstances do shape behavior. It's not without reason that Christ taught us to pray, "Lead us not into temptation."

I'm not exactly sure how this could work to increase public witness.

It's a bit harder to change the whole world so as to make the climate more sympathetic to our testimony of God's love. But perhaps Christ's parable of the sower gives us a clue. Some soils are more receptive than others. People too. We could try to place our friend in a situation where people aren't openly hostile to the gospel. There's a good chance he'll speak up if his potential hearers are already melted to his ideas. We can also encourage him to get in groups where sharing your personal beliefs is the accepted thing to do. This was the reason I signed up for my first speech course in college. I was having trouble telling others what Christ meant to me and I thought the required speeches might provide a structured way of proclaiming God's love. They did.

FOLLOW ME THROUGH. These were the favorite words of my flight instructor when I was learning to control an airplane. He'd place my hand lightly on the control stick, describe the maneuver he was about to perform, and then say, "Follow me through." I learned to fly that way—by imitation. I tried to copy whatever he did. Monkey see, monkey do.

It's sometimes scary to see how quickly others will pick up our behavior pattern. I had a teaching assistant who began to sound like me when he lectured, right down to slang expressions and mannerisms. This shouldn't surprise us. New behavior is caught more than taught. I was the only teaching model he had to go on. We can be effective change agents by being willing to demonstrate openly the behavior we want others to acquire. Jesus said, "Be perfect as I am perfect." Paul told his converts to be imitators of him as he was of Christ.

It's easy to see how this can work in the area of verbal witness. We don't just tell another that he has a responsibility to spread the gospel, sing one chorus of "Pass It On," and send him out into the cold. We go with him. Or better yet, we have him go with us and see how we do it. We provide a living model. It's harder to provide that positive visual model in the realm of sexual conduct. The situation of the person we're trying to influence may be very different from our own. And besides, physical expression of love usually takes place in a private setting. But at least we can take care that we don't become a negative model. Word quickly gets around.

A behavioral model lets the other person know that the action is pos-

"Oh, my goodness! I see you seated at your typewriter... and... and... you're writing another book. I see it becoming the nation's number one best seller. Why, it's a book about me and my uncanny ability to predict the future!"

sible. It offers the neophyte instruction on how to perform it. And it assures him that he'll have company if he does it. If you only want someone to know—tell them. If you want them to do—show them.

TELLING IT LIKE YOU WANT IT TO BE. Messiness was a problem at a Chicago inner city school.[28] Kids littered the floor with gum wrappers, crumpled up school papers, and Kleenex tissues. They showed a casual unconcern when teachers appealed for tidiness. The principal decided to have a clean-up campaign. She came to one class and offered rewards of candy to the kids if they'd shape up the classroom. Things got a little better, but not much. Ironically, when they did win some incentive goodies, the wrappers were found strewn around the room. She tried a different tack with another class. Instead of trying to persuade them to change their messy ways, she simply went before them and announced how pleased she was that they were working hard to keep the room neat. Now understand that the two classes were equally grubby. An actual rubbish check showed that they started out on an equal footing. But whereas she told the first group they were sloppy and needed to clean up, she told the second that they were relatively neat and that she hoped they'd keep up the good work. Within a few weeks they actually did become much neater.

This technique is called attribution. Rather than telling it like it is, you tell it like you want it to be. You attribute to another person the behavior you'd like to encourage. It's a positive approach. Instead of pointing out a person's lack and urging him to change, you publicly assume that he's already doing what you want—and praise him for it. Another term for the approach is "self-fulfilling prophecy." The mere fact that you state that a thing is so actually helps it come to pass. This can break both ways. Tell Johnny that he's always selfish toward his sister and watch the petty acts of rivalry increase. Let him know that you've noticed how considerate of her he often is, and enjoy the upcoming harmony.

You can quickly figure out how to apply attribution procedures in our two areas of illustration. Instead of making a person feel ashamed that he doesn't witness enough, let him know that you're impressed with his willingness to always put in a good word for the Lord. Instead of dragging a man through his sins of the flesh, point out the times he's exhibited commendable self-control. In the words of an old song:

You've got to accentuate the positive,
Eliminate the negative,
Latch on to the affirmative,
*Don't mess with mister in-between.**

"It never fails to get me a seat on the bus."

Is this honest? Is it legitimate to praise a guy for his courage to proclaim the faith when in reality he never says boo to a ghost? Is it right to affirm a man's sexual purity when he's actually on the make? No, of course not. If the situation's that clear-cut, it's wrong to pretend otherwise, but things are rarely that black and white. Usually our behavior is mixed. Some things we do push us one way, other acts pull us in an opposite direction. It seems both prudent and loving to be a mirror which reflects back the praiseworthy actions of others. If we let him know that we see these acts as typical of his dominant nature, we're likely to observe more Christian conduct in the future. Words have power. Saying it's so can make it so.

CLOSING THE SALE. A salesman cares much more about behavior than he does about attitude. He gets no credit for customers' warm positive feelings toward his product. He collects a commission only when they sign on the dotted line. This fact of life has led to some abuses—salesmen trying to trick the buyer, or riding roughshod over his honest objection. But the focus on action has also produced a considerable body of knowledge about why presentations fizzle. Most studies come up with the same answer with almost boring regularity. As strange as it may sound, the reason for most sales flops is that the salesman never gets around to asking the person to buy. He doesn't close the sale. He either avoids or forgets to ask the customer for a specific action. That's why sales manuals constantly come back to the ABC's of persuasion: *A*lways *B*e *C*losing.

If you want others to perform a certain action, don't keep them guessing about what it is. Invite them to participate in certain terms. I saw the wisdom of this when I took part in an effort to recruit donors for a blood drive at a large university. The campuswide response was 2 percent of the student body. I tried to improve on this ratio by presenting a speech on the benefits of blood donation to a random sample of 100 men and women. A post-speech questionnaire showed that their attitude toward donation was positively affected. They thought it was a great idea. The problem was that only two of the hearers actually gave a pint. With this group I didn't beat the campus average.

I did something else with 100 other students. I presented the same speech and then tacked on a specific appeal for action. After passing out donor cards, I told them exactly how to sign up for an appointment. I stressed the action implications of a favorable attitude toward blood contribution. The donor records revealed that six of these students volunteered. That's not a whopping improvement, but it's a half gallon more than we would have gotten if I hadn't pressed for specific action. I also checked this second group's response on the attitude questionnaire and made an interesting discovery. The ninety-four people who declined to give had a very cynical reaction toward the value of blood donation. They were much more negative than those in the group who heard only the speech. Apparently a person can be favorable in attitude without acting as long as he hasn't had a choice confrontation. But once the specific behavior is spelled out and he decides not to do it, the attitude plummets. As we saw earlier, attitudes follow behavior.

The practice of setting forth specific behavioral objectives is commonplace in education and industry, but is relatively new in Christian evangelism. It means listing concrete action that the witness can take—mentioning Jesus Christ when anybody asks where he goes to church, making one call a week in a church visitation program, broaching the subject of faith with his next-door neighbor. Notice that these goals don't involve the second person's response, they just describe the initial action. An effective program of behavioral objectives will set realistic goals for each actor. Remember those who didn't give blood when asked. If the cost sets the hurdle too high, the person will trip and fall—taking his attitude with him.

The whole subject of sexual conduct screams out for concrete discussion. We're used to talking in vague terms that end up confusing rather than clarifying. I find that adolescents are desperately seeking some guidelines on what to do. Just this week a fellow asked, "How far can I go?" I responded with, "How far do you want to go?" This was embarrassing, and obviously dirty pool. His face got red and he looked away. Finally he mumbled, "Aw, you know, Em." But that's precisely the problem—I didn't know for sure, and he didn't know what was appropriate for a Christian. We had to get down to specifics:

Nothing wrong with holding hands, is there?
How about putting an arm around her shoulders?
Is kissing OK?
What about a long body-length embrace?

Is it ever all right to touch her breast?
What if . . .?

Unless you're willing to call a spade a spade, you'll have very little influence on dating behavior. You need to be willing to lay concrete practices out on the table where they can be discussed and examined. Then close the sale. Make a specific request.

FOOT-IN-THE-DOOR. Sometimes what we're asking another to do is such a whopping change in behavior that it's really inconceivable to him that he could make the shift. The total abandonment of one set of responses and the complete adoption of another set seems much too radical. Better that we move him along the road in that direction by small increments. A journey of a thousand miles begins with one small step.

The effectiveness of the step-by-step technique was demonstrated in a famous real life study known as the foot-in-the-door experiment.[29] The researchers selected a number of homes at random and made personal visits to the residents. They claimed to represent an environmental group which was erecting billboards that said, KEEP CALIFORNIA BEAUTIFUL. They asked whether or not the homeowners would be willing to display this sign on their front lawn. In order to insure that residents fully understood the request, they showed them a picture of a similar house with the sign in front. It was really quite funny. Here's an ugly six-by-ten-foot billboard defacing the property while urging others to beautify the state. The idea that anybody would actually choose to put up such a monstrosity seemed patently ridiculous. And it was—no one accepted the offer.

The researchers used a two-step procedure with another group of homeowners in order to test out the foot-in-the-door technique. They first went to the residents with a small three-by-five-inch card and asked people to stick it in their window. The card contained the same appeal for state beautification. Because the behavioral cost of displaying the modest sign was low, many people did it. This left the door open to a much larger request later on. A few weeks later the callers came back to the folks who had accepted the small sign. They presented their request for permission to put up the huge billboard. Although the majority of the people refused, quite a few agreed to take the large sign.

How can we explain this difference? The simplest answer is that the men and women who put up the first message began to view themselves differently. They observed their own behavior just as anyone else would. What they saw was a person who was concerned about the environment. Here was a man who was willing to let his friends and neighbors know the importance of protecting the state's natural splendor. They were reminded of their own commitment to conservation every time they saw the sign.

What we have here could be called persuasion through self-perception.[30] A person becomes convinced by watching his own action. This gives him the impetus to clear behavior hurdles he'd have tripped over before. Given bite-sized increases and enough time, he may eventually be able to leap tall buildings in a single bound. As Jesus said when his disciples chastised a man for casting out demons in his name, "Do not forbid him; for no one who does a mighty work in my name will be able soon after to speak evil of me" (Mark 9:39).

We can use the foot-in-the-door approach to get people to regard themselves as bold witnesses for Christ instead of scared Christians who are ashamed of their faith. The secret lies in not expecting too much at the start. If we dangle the great heroes of the faith in front of them as a model, they'll become discouraged and back off completely. But if we start out by encouraging them to do relatively easy acts of witness, they'll be successful and build up confidence as they go along. The line-up of hurdles on page 181 serves as a good example. It would be a mistake to expect this man to share his faith with his boss if the cost loomed that large. Since sending a religious Christmas card poses no such threat, he can start there and work up.

I've known of the same method being used to help a Christian break off an illicit sexual relationship. A young married woman came to her pastor and confessed that she was having intercourse regularly with another man. She knew this was wrong and wanted to stop, but was devastated at the idea of never seeing the man again. The minister decided to make a contract with her. She agreed to cut back the number of times they got together to once a week. This she could handle. After three weeks they changed the terms of the contract. She'd sleep with the man only once a month. By this time she began to see the light at the

"I love you! I love you! I love you! By George, I think I've gone and convinced myself."

end of the tunnel. She could cope with life without this man. Three months after first coming to the pastor, the woman severed the relationship.

Many of us may be tempted to raise an eyebrow or look askance at this counseling technique. We'd feel better if the pastor had said, "Go home, sin no more. God will give you the strength." But this could have driven her from the faith and crushed her emotionally. She was receiving precious little love from her husband. The thought of losing her main source of human warmth was terrifying. By programming a gradual withdrawal the pastor helped her build up a confidence and ability to do without this man. It was probably the pastor's flexibility which allowed her to come to him in the first place.

* * * *

By now you're probably sick and tired of figuring out ways to stimulate Christians to verbalize their faith or modify their sexual conduct. But I hope these examples have helped you to understand different ways of influencing behavior. Don't rely solely on attitude change. Our actions often fly in the face of our feelings and beliefs. Give some thought to these five proven techniques:

1. Don't try to change the person—change the situation.
2. Don't tell him what to do—show him.
3. Don't knock his present actions—attribute to him the response you desire.
4. Don't speak in generalities—get specific as to what he should do.
5. Don't expect too much change at one time—request minor behavior shifts.

14

Conformity

Let's start this chapter with a test of visual perception. Take a look at these lines. Which line—A, B or C—is the same length as line X?

It doesn't seem that tough, does it? If you're like 99 percent of the people who see the diagram by themselves, you'll answer line A. And you'd be right. It's hard to imagine anyone missing something so obvious, isn't it?

But suppose you weren't alone when you saw the lines. Imagine instead that you are part of a group of twelve people, and that each of them announces his decision before it's your turn. When the first person names line C you almost laugh out loud. How can he be so stupid? Then the second group member also picks line C as equal in length to line X. You simply can't believe it. Barnum said that there was one born every minute, but here are two of them right in the same room. After the third member agrees with the first two, you begin to rub your eyes. Are they seeing something different than you? Maybe you should get your eyes checked.

As each successive person announces line C as his judgment, you feel a growing confusion. You're positive that line A is the right answer—at least you were. Yet all of the others seem equally certain that you're wrong. What will they say when you oppose them—if you do? Will they laugh as you were tempted to do a moment earlier? Or will they sit there tolerantly with only a flicker of a smile to hint at their contempt for a person as weird as you? After the rest of the group has unanimously chosen line C, they all turn their eyes on you and ask for your decision. If you were in this situation, what would you say?

The people who had to make this decision were taking part in an experiment on conformity. Unknown to them, the other eleven people were paid confederates instructed to agree on the wrong answer. This placed the lone individual in an isolated position where he would feel a strong pressure to conform to the rest of the group. The procedure was devised by a researcher named Solomon Asch to test the question of whether or not people would ignore the plain evidence of their senses and cave in under group pressure.[31] Over one-third of the folks did give in and swing to the side of the majority. In a dramatic way this experiment confirmed what we observe in our everyday life. People in a group feel pressure to bring their actions and thoughts into line with other members of the group.

Perhaps a few examples are in order. The other night my son announced that he was going to sell his bike. Since he usually rides it a mile and a half to school each day I asked why. "Oh, Dad, *nobody* rides a bike to school anymore," he responded. Those of you who are parents will smile at the familiar sound of hearing that nobody does something, or its equally prevalent counterpart—that everyone does it. Before I knock the conformity behavior of my children, however, I need to come to grips with my own tendencies to follow the crowd. A few years ago I gave away all my white dress shirts when it suddenly dawned on me that my colleagues wore only colors, patterns, and stripes. And just the other day I arrived "fashionably late" at a faculty meeting because I expected the majority of professors to do likewise.

It's popular to decry the low level of individuality and autonomy among our present generation. Some American writers claim that we

"You're a disgrace to all lemmings!"

are a nation of sheep, uncritically following the dictates of business and political leaders. Others complain about the "mindless conformity" of the masses. But these protests are too simplistic. They're based on the notion that it's always wrong to adapt your ideas or actions to the judgments of the group. The writer of Proverbs makes no such assumption. "Where there is no guidance, a people falls; but in an abundance of counselors there is safety" (Proverbs 11:14). And again, "Without counsel plans go wrong, but with many advisers they succeed" (Proverbs 15:22). As this ancient wisdom suggests, there are times when it's folly to fly in the face of majority opinion. We have a modern tongue-in-cheek parable which states the same thing: "If you can keep your head while others around you are losing theirs, it's obvious you don't understand the situation.''

The easy popular criticism of conformity also assumes that the man who follows the crowd in one instance will automatically do so in another situation. But it just isn't so! You'll recall that one-third of the people switched to the wrong answer in the initial line-judgment experiment. Further research has shown that it's possible to rig the situation so that almost everyone conforms to the group's answer. It's equally possible to alter the set-up so that no one conforms. The difference is not in personality, but in situation. Some conditions encourage a person to weigh his own perceptions and experience heavily, while almost ignoring the thoughts and desires of those around him.[32] In this case—no conformity. But change some of the situational factors and that very same man will tend to doubt the value of his own judgment and rely almost totally on the opinion of those around him.

As Christian persuaders we need to know those situational factors. On the negative side, we want to avoid placing anyone in such a strong group pressure situation that they simply can't say no to our message. This would be dishonoring to the Lord and show a casual disregard for them as fellow human beings. We also want to be able to spot those non-Christian group situations where the cards are stacked so high that believers will have a tough time maintaining their faith and witness. Again, it's not without reason that Christ taught us to pray, ''Lead us not into temptation.''

On the positive side, there are times when the support and encouragement of the group can help a new convert solidify his newfound faith. Group expectations can give backbone to a tentative commitment. The writer of Hebrews parades the heroes of the faith by his reader in the eleventh chapter and then makes his conformity appeal: ''Therefore, since we are surrounded by so great a cloud of witnesses, let us . . .run with perseverance the race that is set before us'' (Hebrews 12:1).

For these reasons, the rest of the chapter will focus on the situational factors that increase pressure towards group uniformity. There are ten different factors. If they all line up together, the pressure to conform can be overwhelming. Of course the reverse is true. If none of them come into play, a person feels absolutely no force to live up to the group's expectation.

1. OVERT REWARDS. In Asch's first experiment, the confederates gave no outward response when the subject announced his answer. They didn't smile if he agreed with the "right" answer, line C, nor did they mock or show disgust if he stuck to his guns and insisted that line A was correct. If there had been this kind of reaction, conformity would have skyrocketed.

Most groups give all sorts of rewards and honors for agreeing with the majority. Smiles, head nods, hugs, friendship, public recognition, prizes, merit badges, and election to leadership are just a few of the positive goodies a group doles out to those who live up to its standards. Overt acclaim or blame is an effective way to keep members in line.

There's a story about a college class that decided to see how much they could affect the prof's lecturing style. Apparently it was a pretty dry class and they had little else to do to occupy their time. Whenever he spoke from the lectern or wandered toward the side of the room by the hall door, they'd do all the little things that teachers find irritating. They'd slouch down in their seats, frown, whisper to one another, chew gum, close their notebooks, and idly watch the traffic go by. Whenever the prof moved to the window side of the room, however, they'd reward him with the response teachers love to see—gazing avidly into his eyes, nodding their heads in agreement, smiling, and taking copious notes. Within two days they had him delivering his entire lecture sitting on the window sill.

The power of visible group sanctions can be awesome and terrible. One morning my daughter joyfully showed me a pair of "high rise" sandals that she'd just bought. They had about an inch of foam rubber under the soles and they really looked quite spiffy. She proudly trooped off to school to show them off. That night I asked her how her friends had liked the shoes. She tearfully told me that she hated the dumb old things—they hurt her feet. Some gentle probing revealed the real reason. Two girls had laughed at her, one said they made her look like a giraffe, and a fourth stated bluntly that Sharon couldn't play ball on her team if she wore the sandals. When a group overtly expresses its reaction to a member's behavior, conformity soars.

2. PUBLIC SCRUTINY. I'm a member of the Faculty Senate at Wheaton College. The college president recently brought a sensitive

proposal to the body for its approval. The discussion lasted for about fifteen minutes and no one spoke out directly against the proposal. A tentative show of hands revealed only one person opposed to the motion. However, he requested a secret written ballot and surprisingly the final vote was 14 yeas and 11 nays. The obvious question is, Why did ten mature adults vote for something publicly but against it privately? The obvious answer is that they felt much less pressure to conform to the "acceptable" position when they could shield their opinion from public view.

When we talk about the effects of social pressure, we've got to realize that there can be a big difference between public compliance and private acceptance. Compliance refers to public statements and outward behavior. Since these are open to outside scrutiny, they're quite susceptible to group influence. Private acceptance is another matter. The group can't monitor what a person believes in his heart-of-hearts. It's not unusual, therefore, to have a person go along with the crowd while maintaining inward reservations.

There are numerous biblical examples of men publicly conforming despite contrary inward feelings. Two of the saddest occur in connection with Jesus' death. In the upper room Peter boldly proclaims his steadfast love for the Lord. We have no reason to doubt that his inward convictions remained constant throughout the following days; yet a few hours later he publicly conformed to the anti-Jesus sentiment in Caiaphas' courtyard. Pilate had no inward desire to execute Jesus, but Scripture makes it plain that he caved into the conformity pressure of the mob. "So Pilate, wishing to satisfy the crowd, released for them Barabbas" (Mark 15:15).

Interestingly enough, there's a clear case of nonconformity occurring a few days later. Jesus rose from the dead and was seen by ten disciples and other followers as well. Despite their strong urging, Thomas chose to reject group opinion and rely entirely on his own senses and direct experience. In his situation Thomas was able to resist the added force to conform which a group member feels when he has to make his position known. In their situation, Peter and Pilate were not.

3. NO TRUE PARTNER

Two are better than one, because they have a good reward for their toil.

"Eleven hamburgers, one frank. Eleven coffees, one tea. Eleven apple pies, one chocolate cake...."

For if they fail, one will lift up his fellow; but woe to him who is alone when he falls and has not another to lift him up. Again, if two lie together, they are warm; but how can one be warm alone? And though a man might prevail against one who is alone, two will withstand him. A threefold cord is not quickly broken (Ecclesiastes 4:9-16).

It's hard to stand alone. John F. Kennedy's book *Profiles in Courage* makes for compelling reading because it sketches the lives of historical figures who withstood the clamor of the majority. Each remained a minority of one in order to preserve the integrity of what they thought was right. We admire such men. We wish that every Christian could stand firm in the midst of a group urging him to ignore his convictions. But let's face it—it's tough.

In the line-judgment experiment, Asch discovered what he called the "true partner effect." He instructed one of his confederates to give the right answer. Although the subject still found ten people disagreeing with him, he also discovered one who supported his view. The difference this made was phenomenal. Almost all of the people who'd caved in when faced with solid opposition now remained firm when accompanied by a true partner.

This finding is mirrored by a dramatic study of long-term persuasion that took thirty years to complete.[33] The study followed the progress of the 1936 freshman class at Bennington College, an exclusive and expensive school for girls. Most of these gals were brought up in conservative Republican homes, and they brought their parents' anti-New Deal attitudes along when they came to school. They were in for a surprise. Bennington was a new experimental school, and most of the professors were young, attractive, articulate—and liberal. Throughout their four years in school, Bennington coeds grew increasingly progressive in their political outlook. By the time they graduated most girls were far to the left of their parents and hometown friends. The big question was, Would they stay that way?

In 1966, all living class graduates were contacted and questioned about their political leanings. Not surprisingly, some maintained their Bennington-inspired liberal views while others had switched back. What was striking was the reason. If a gal married a liberal fellow, she maintained her liberal attitudes. If she didn't find this kind of true partner, she reverted to her original conservative position.

The lack of one close person to agree with you can be devastating in religion as well as politics. I've seen many high school fellows and gals become Christians. I'm constantly surprised by those who are around the faith five to ten years later. Some who I thought were true rocks have long since thrown over their initial belief. Others who were very tentative are now pillars of the faith. The one thing that seems to have made the difference is who they married. If they found a Christian mate, they're around and active. If they didn't, they just drift away. Paul said it: "Don't be unequally yoked with an unbeliever."

It may be true that "one man with God is a majority." But if that man has one other close friend who shares his opinion, he can more easily withstand the non-Christian pressure of those who surround him. Without such a true partner, the pressure to conform can be almost irresistible. It's not without reason that Jesus sent the disciples out two by two.

4. ATTRACTION TO THE GROUP. I became a Christian because of an attractive group of people. It was at the beginning of my senior year in high school. I'd always run around with kids a year or so older than me. The problem, of course, was that they all graduated by the end of my junior year. I was drawn to a mixed bunch of eight or nine guys and gals. Sarcasm had always been the big thing in my school and most students continually cut one another down. But these kids really seemed to like one another. What's more, they appeared to like me.

Because of their attractiveness, I began to do things they wanted. It turned out they were Christians and they asked me to go on a weekend retreat. Now ordinarily I would've said no, since it fell at the same time as the first fall football game. That may not sound like such a big deal, but I'd never missed seeing a game my whole school career. It was the "in" thing to do. But since I wanted to be accepted by the group, I passed up the game and went off with them on the retreat.

Because of their attractiveness, I also accepted ideas which would have put me off in another situation. I can remember all of us sitting together on a sand dune and one gal suggesting that we go around and quote our favorite Bible verse. Ordinarily this would have grossed me out. I didn't even know any passages in the Bible, much less have memorized one. The only time I had ever opened the book was to press a leaf collection for my sophomore biology class. But because I admired them, this seemed a reasonable thing to do rather than some far-out exercise. They didn't even make me feel uncomfortable when I haltingly told them I'd like to pass when it came my turn.

I became a Christian that weekend. I did so because I'd fallen into a highly attractive group of people. I decided that I wanted to be like them. Whatever it was they had, I was going to have. Since they had Jesus Christ, I accepted him too. I think if they'd been Buddhists I'd have joined Youth for Buddha on the spot.

Perhaps this doesn't strike you as the most noble reason for entering the faith. But God has used attractive fellowships to draw people to himself since the day of Pentecost.

And all who believed were together and had all things in common; and they sold their possessions and goods and distributed them to all, as any had need. And day by day, attending the temple together and breaking bread in their homes, they partook of food with glad and generous hearts, praising God and having favor with all the people. And the Lord added to their number day by day those who were being saved (Acts 2:44-47).

The first-century world looked at the church and said, "Behold how they love one another," and they came to join in droves.

The more attractive a group is to its members, the greater the influence it'll have on them. A warm, close-knit group is particularly potent because it employs a "friendly persuasion." It doesn't have to use force. As comedian Dick Gregory puts it: "If you really live your beliefs and make them attractive, you don't have to ram your ideas down other people's throats—they will steal them."

5. COMMITMENT TO CONTINUE. I was walking by a park the other day when I overheard a group of boys engaged in a hot argument. It seems they were about to play a baseball game and the entire group wanted a boy named Jeff to play right field. This caught my attention because it's the story of my baseball career—I was always the one left over to play right field. But Jeff refused to knuckle under to the group will. He ultimately resorted to the classic response: "Then I won't play. I'm going home." And he did.

This story illustrates the limitations of group pressure. Conformity force can never be stronger than an individual's commitment to stay with the group. As long as he has the real option of picking up and leaving, he can afford to ignore the group's expectations. But if the situation is such that he's compelled to deal with these same folks over and over again in the future, the group's demands can be well nigh irresistible.

I once served on our church's pulpit committee. Our minister had left to take another church, and it was our job to come up with a suitable successor. There were six men and six women on the committee. Each person represented a different segment of our 1500-member congregation. The job of getting these twelve varied representatives to agree on any one candidate appeared insurmountable. It was only our commitment to continue which brought us to a unanimous decision.

The congregation instructed us to meet weekly until we selected a new pastor. Over a span of seven months, we reviewed ninety dossiers, heard twenty-five recorded sermons, and personally interviewed ten men. After all this, the committee was split in its opinion. Nine members were vigorously in favor of calling a dynamic man in his early thirties. The other three were equally opposed to his selection due to his inexperience. The pressure upon those three to change their minds was fierce. One man told me he was so tired of receiving invitations to lunch, phone calls, and dirty looks that he could scream. He considered holding out against the majority just for spite, but like the two others, he came over in the end. He put it this way later. "I realized that if I held out and voted no, I'd have to face the same people again next Monday night and start all over. Somehow I just couldn't face that."

It's easy to criticize those who give up their own convictions for those of the majority. But standard conformity theory suggests that there are just three options open to those who feel the pressure toward uniformity. They can leave the group, change the others, or change themselves. If the circumstances are such that they *can't* leave the group, the pressure's really on. The truth of this can be seen in the conformity of an Army barracks, the gang rule of prison life, or the low tolerance for deviance in remote rural communities. Whether it comes about through external force or voluntary compact, commitment to continue promotes conformity.

6. STATUS DIFFERENCE. While I'm writing this I have one eye on the TV set. I'm watching the U. S. Open Golf Tournament, and the faces of Jack Nicklaus, Johnny Miller, and Arnold Palmer are flashing by on the screen. Suppose I was in a group of these men and we were discussing the best way of fading a three wood to the green from a downhill lie. Do you think I'd be likely to stick with my uneducated

opinion when confronted with the wisdom of these men? No way! I'd shut up, listen, and learn. I'd be low man on the totem pole in such a group, and quick to adopt the majority decision.

In other groups, however, I feel quite confident that my opinion is as good as—if not better than—the next guy's. I'm serving on a school committee which has the responsibility of planning faculty meetings. The other five members all agreed that faculty discussion groups should have about twelve to fifteen members. Having some expertise in the field of group dynamics, I felt free to voice my opinion that seven was a more wieldy size, and I was able to stand firm in the face of initial opposition.

We see then that status is a relative thing. I may be held in high regard in one group and thought of as an idiot in another. It's also topic bound. I may feel competent in some areas—persuasion, small plane aviation, and swimming come to mind—and be a complete dolt concerning other topics—auto mechanics, geology, and oil painting to name just a few. As a fellow professor puts it, we're all laymen in every subject except one.

Note that status is a subjective thing. In conformity it doesn't matter how competent I really am, just how sharp I *think* I am. Expertise is in the eye of the beholder. If I feel I know more than others in the group, I'll be willing to deviate from the group norm. If, however, I feel inferior to others, the pressure to conform will be great.

We might take a look at group leadership in this context. The popular leader often has high status. This frees him from the conformity pressure that his followers experience and allows him to try new and different things. He can deviate from the group's standard—be creative. But there's a paradox here. He achieved his high esteem in the first place by conforming more to the group's expectations than anybody else. If it's a horseshoe club, he throws more ringers. If it's a PTA committee, he's shown that he cares more about kids' education. And if it's a Bible study fellowship, he's demonstarted a superior knowledge of Scripture. It's as if he's built up "acceptance capital" by conforming. He can now spend some of that capital to be independent of the group's wishes. He just needs to make sure he doesn't spend the bank account dry by deviating too much and too often.

"Well, heck! If all you smart cookies agree, who am I to dissent?"

7. LARGE DISCREPANCY. I went to college at the University of Michigan in the late 1950s. After a few weeks on campus, I pledged a fraternity. To be honest, I'm not even sure I considered God's will in the matter; I'd just always assumed that this was the route to go. My grandfather was one of the charter members of that particular house at Michigan, my father had joined a fraternity at a different school, and all my high school friends planned to become Greeks as well. It seemed the normal thing to do.

I soon discovered that this attitude wasn't shared by Christians on campus. Among over 100 members of the Michigan Christian Fellowship, I was the only one to belong to a fraternity. Their questions and comments made it clear that some regarded my decision as somewhat strange, while the others considered it downright immoral. The clear-cut discrepancy between my behavior and the group's expectation really put me through the wringer. I felt a strong pressure from the fellowship to reconsider my house membership—to comply with their non-Greek example.

We also had another area of disagreement. No one in the evangelical fellowship smoked. They had the conviction that it was wrong. As a matter of fact, I didn't smoke either. But my stance wasn't because I regarded smoking as sinful; I merely believed that it was a messy habit which would slow me down in my competitive swimming. Although I shared my view with the rest of the group and triggered considerable disagreement, I received very little hassle from other members to bring my opinion into line with theirs. Why? Because the discrepancy between my position and theirs was small. If I actually smoked, however, it would've been a different matter—like that of fraternity membership.

We can see, therefore, that the greater the discrepancy between an individual's position and the one held by the group, the more pressure he'll feel to change his mind.

8. HIGH RELEVANCE TO GROUP GOAL. In another chapter I mentioned that I'm a hockey nut. I'm not alone. Whenever I go to Jim's games there are sixteen other dads who are equally involved. Since we're tossed together at least once a week for the better part of a year, we've developed into a rather close-knit group. During this time I've discovered that most of these men have extremely conservative social views—perhaps a little to the right of slavery. Since my own views toward education, race relations, government fiscal matters, and foreign policy tend to be more liberal, I've found myself at odds with them more than once. But I've never picked up signals that they expect me to change my opinions. Why? Because my attitude toward prison reform has little to do with the reason for our association—hockey. Let our discussion touch on matters relevant to hockey though, and it's a different story.

Of the seventeen boys on the team, only six can play at any one time. I happen to believe that all boys should get equal ice time. To me, the whole purpose of the league is to give our kids a chance to try out their skills in keen competition, have some strenuous exercise, and make new friends. I'm a very competitive guy and like to win, but the fun goes out of the whole thing when some of the guys are sitting on the

bench night after night. Jim plays more than most, so this isn't just a
"sour grapes" attitude.

The majority of the fathers do not share this outlook. They state their
position bluntly, if not originally: "Winning's the name of the game.
It's not the main thing, it's the only thing. If you aren't going to play to
win, why keep score?" These men are uncomfortable with my attitude.
It's a threat to their position, and they work hard to change my mind. If
one of the better players scores a goal, a dad is sure to nudge me and
observe that it wouldn't have happened had the good player been off the
ice. He's also likely to point out how happy the fellows on the bench are
that the team is winning.

Because my deviant opinion is highly relevant to the goal of our
group, I receive lots of pressure to change my view. Group members
are much more tolerant of a strange idea when it doesn't touch upon
their very purpose for being together.

9. LACK OF PRIOR COMMITMENT TO THE ISSUE. There's a
bittersweet story about a West Virginia mountain boy who was drafted
into the army. The fellow had been raised in a small secluded church
and he and all the other church members worried that exposure to the
world would cause him to lose his faith. They held an all-night prayer
vigil on his behalf the night before he left for boot camp. The boy didn't
write home at all during his two-year hitch in the service, so it was with
considerable interest that the whole fellowship gathered around him
when he returned. "How'd it go?" they asked. "Were you able to hold
onto your faith?" The young man responded enthusiastically, "You
know, I was really scared. But your prayers helped and it turned out just
great. I was in the Army the whole two years and nobody ever found out
I was a Christian!"

Of course this story is sad because God doesn't want us to conceal
our Christian convictions. He wants our love for him to be contagious.
But the story also suggests that the boy from the hills spent two years
conforming to the standards of the other guys in the barracks. A strong
public stand on an issue makes a person resistant to social pressure in
the opposite direction. He'll lose face if he switches. A low level of
commitment to a position leaves a person wide open to group influence.

It was public knowledge in my college fraternity that Em Griffin didn't drink. This was unusual behavior, and unfortunately I made such a big deal out of it that the other guys equated my Christian stance with not drinking. I experienced a great deal of kidding, arguing, and even downright hostility from my fraternity brothers in an effort to get me to "bend an elbow" with them. But since I was publicly committed to abstinence, it made it easy to withstand the group pressure. Some of the fellows later told me that they secretly hoped I wouldn't give in.

On the other hand, I did readily conform in another matter. I'm a morning person, not a night owl. I like to hit the sack early. This desire ran counter to the house norm, which was to stay up well past midnight. The issue wasn't *that* important to me, and I never publicly announced my opinion that the group's sleeping habits were unreasonable. Because of my low commitment to the issue, I soon found myself sliding into the normal pattern of the house and yawned my way through the day.

The man who is highly committed to a point of view would rather fight than switch. The one who sees the issue as relatively unimportant will tend to give in. The most often heard explanation for conformity behavior is: "I just didn't think it was worth arguing about."

10. UNCERTAINTY. Look back at the line-judgment test at the start of the chapter. The thing that makes conformity surprising in this instance is that the right answer is so obvious, so certain. But what if the difference in length were much smaller? What if you were asked to pick out the line below that has a length equal to line X on page 193? This situation gets pretty ambiguous, and it would take a very independent person to stick to his guns if he knew that everyone else agreed on a different answer.

A _____
B _____
C _____

We all have a need to compare our deeds and opinions with those of others who are similar to us. We want to make certain that we don't do anything foolish. The fuzzier the situation is, the more we depend upon someone else's observations and judgment to define appropriate behavior. It follows that a completely ambiguous social situation might well produce total conformity. A pioneer research project confirms this prediction.[34]

A volunteer was placed in a totally dark room. After he was seated, the experimenter called his attention to a small pinprick of light on one wall. He told the volunteer that the light would soon move. He asked him to stare at the light and to estimate how far it traveled. Actually the light never moves, it just looks like it does. This is known as the "auto-kinetic effect." A stationary light in an all black field will appear to drift if you gaze at it for more than a few seconds. People varied widely on the distance they thought the light traveled when they viewed it by themselves. Some said one half inch. Others thought two feet was about right. When three or four of these subjects were brought together to view the light at the same time, they quickly adjusted their estimates so that they'd cluster together in a very narrow range. Some groups arrived at consistent judgments of three inches. Other foursomes coalesced around answers of about a foot. But all groups quickly developed norms which influenced their future judgments.

This study points out the desperate need we have for some objective reality. In the absence of an outside frame of reference, man will become what Jude calls a waterless cloud, being blown hither and yon depending on which group blows the hardest. The experiment highlights the fantastic treasure we have in the plumb line of Scripture, which is our "only rule for faith and practice." The problem is, of course, that to most people the whole question of religion is extremely ambiguous. They can't see God, so how do they know he exists? It rains on the bad man's fields as well as on the crops of a good man, so how can they be certain that God rewards those that seek him? As a result, most people are tremendously influenced in their theological beliefs by those that surround them. Uncertainty leads to conformity.

The autokinetic experiment confirmed another fact of significance to Christians—the influence of a group norm lasts long after the originators of the standard have left the group. The experimenter checked this by running a number of trials with a constantly changing group. Before each run he'd remove one group member and add a new one. Let me illustrate. Suppose that Andy, Bill, and Chad are confederates who pretend that the light moves ten inches. Dave, the naive fourth member, quickly adopts their judgment. In the next trial, Andy drops out and Eric joins the group. Eric, like Dave and all the others who participate later, has no idea that the original three men were in cahoots, and he's influenced by the standard they set. In the next trial Bill drops out and Fred enters the group. In the one after that, Chad leaves and Gene comes in. Note that at this point, all of the confederates are gone; yet the newcomers still alter their original perception to conform to the group consensus, which stays close to ten inches for each successive generation. The experiment is diagrammed below. You can see that Ned has never met Andy, Bill, or Chad. Yet he unknowingly adjusts his opinion to get closer to the ten-inch standard they established long before. The startling fact is that the influence of the original group still holds sway ten generations later. This calls to mind the statement in the Decalogue that God "visits the sins of the fathers upon the children to the third and the fourth generation of those that hate him." Any way you slice it, group influence is a powerful force.

AUTOKINETIC EXPERIMENT OVER GENERATIONS

Participants (Andy, Bill & Chad are confederates)

1	*Andy Bill Chad* Dave
2	*Bill Chad* Dave Eric
3	*Chad* Dave Eric Fred
4	Dave Eric Fred Gene
5	Eric Fred Gene Harv
6	Fred Gene Harv Irv
7	Gene Harv Irv Jack
8	Harv Irv Jack King
9	Irv Jack King Lou
10	Jack King Lou Mark
11	King Lou Mark Ned

Generation

* * * *

I like to think of these ten factors as engaged in a type of conformity tug-of-war. If the situation is such that five of them encourage dependence on the group and five self-reliance, it's chancy to speculate on whether or not a person will conform. However, if eight, nine, or ten of the factors line up together on the social pressure end of the rope, conformity is a foregone conclusion.

Every fall I teach a group dynamics course on an island in Lake Michigan. For two weeks I'm isolated with eight college students. Since we can't get away from each other, there's a strong *Commitment to continue*. Soccer is the big game on the island. Because I break the class into two four-member teams, it's not just recreation, it's also *relevant to the purpose* of the group. Last year I had one gal who was a freshman, while all the others were upperclassmen. She was quite *attracted* to the others—especially the guys. They had all played soccer before, whereas she was a novice. In both age and experience they had a *status* advantage over her.

Having never played before, she was *uncertain* what kind of footwear was appropriate—in fact she'd never thought about it before. She came to the not unreasonable conclusion that she'd be able to kick the ball farther by wearing heavy hiking boots. Her decision was easily *open to public scrutiny*. You couldn't help but notice those clodhoppers. And they proved to be *highly discrepant* from the lightweight tennis shoes chosen by the rest of the group. She was the only one wearing boots, she had *no true partner*. Her teammates were afraid she couldn't run well in them. Her opponents were afraid of being kicked in the shins. Therefore, they made it clear they wouldn't let her play unless she changed shoes (*Overt reward*).

Once you understand this whole situation, you don't have to be a prophet or the son of a prophet to predict what she did. As a matter of fact, she set a world's record in changing from hiking boots to P. F. Flyers.

It's possible for the situation to weigh heavily on the deviancy side of the tug-of-war rope. You might see this if you can call to mind a personal instance when all factors favored individuality. Have you ever been thrown together with a group of people you don't especially like and will never see again? You happen to be an expert on the topic under discussion, and it's an area where it's easy to decide what's right. You've been privately committed to your position for a long time, and there's at least one other fellow in the group who sees things your way. Your way of thinking isn't that far from the majority opinion, and besides, it's just a bull session—nobody really knows or cares that you don't agree with them. If you've ever been in a group under those circumstances, it's a safe bet you held to your own opinion.

So we see that group pressure is situational. There are times when it can be an irresistible force. There are other circumstances which can make the individual an immovable object. The ethical persuader needs to understand and respect this fact. The question is not whether a person will conform—but when he'll conform, or even more important, to whom?

Shakespeare said that the world is a stage and we, the people, are mere players. I've been on stage enough to realize that the player isn't acting in isolation. The audience affects his performance. Applause encourages him to do whatever he's been doing, only more so. Stony silence will stimulate him to change—to try something different. It's the same in real life. We play out our lives before an audience. These people can shake us up with disapproval or confirm our actions with praise. The vital question is: To what audience shall we play our lives?

Paul says, "Don't let the world around you squeeze you into its own mould" (Romans 12:2, *Phillips*). It sounds like he's denouncing all conformity. But then he adds, "Let God re-mould your minds from within. . . ." Every human being is going to be squeezed, molded, and shaped by others. The crucial issue is—which others? The non-Christian chooses to play his life to an audience of the world. The Christian is one who has decided to place God and his saints in the audience. He's playing his life in response to Christ and his church. The implications for the Christian persuader are clear.

We must help the one who is young in the faith by surrounding him with others who are sympathetic to the gospel of Jesus Christ. Through counsel and example, we can aid him to self-select groups of friends who'll provide warm encouragement for the faith without smothering him with their own stringent rules or expectations. In fact, that's not a bad idea for us as well. We need to make sure that our own audience is packed with those who have the loving mind of Christ. This kind of social support can firm us up in our commitment to the point where we can say with the tree planted by the river, "I shall not be moved."

15

Burning the Candle at Both Ends

We're used to thinking of persuasion as a one-way process. Someone does something to someone else. The picture that springs to mind is a hunter training his rifle on some big game. This imagery creeps into our persuasive terminology. We talk about persuasive aims, bringing up the big guns, saving the best shot for last, and focusing in on the target audience. The title of the second chapter shows that it's tough to shake free from this marksmanship model. The problem with the analogy, however, is that it lulls us into believing that the persuader can stand aloof and be unaffected by what he does. He can't. Influence is a two-way street. If I get close enough to you to have an impact on your life, there's an equal opportunity for you to sway me. Chances are that a little bit of both will happen.

I've called this final chapter, ''Burning the Candle at Both Ends.'' This picks up the candle-making imagery that has provided the organizational scheme for the book. Not only is persuasion a process of melting, molding, and making hard—it also involves getting wax on our hands. The dramatic arts are full of illustrations of how the persuader is affected by his efforts to persuade. In the Broadway musical *My Fair Lady*, Henry Higgins sets out to turn a common street girl into a lady. He thought he could change Liza Doolittle's life without being affected

Copyright © 1971. Reprinted by permission of Saturday Review and Wm. Hoest.

himself. In a delightful fashion the audience is shown that this is impossible. Arthur Miller's sobering play *Death of a Salesman* makes the same point. We see the tragic person of Willy Loman slowly disintegrate before our eyes. His unsuccessful attempts to move others have a snowballing impact on his life.

There are many by-products of Christian influence. One is the feeling of euphoria that comes from helping someone find life in Jesus Christ. As John puts it in his first letter, "We tell you these things that our joy may be full." If the angels can get excited about this, so can we. Another side effect of Christian persuasion is a growing commitment to the cause of Christ. The very activity of telling others about God, requesting dollars for his church, or encouraging others to do good things can deepen our resolve to serve the Lord. But in this chapter I'd like to look at a different area—one we don't often think about. I'm going to focus on the unintended effects of persuasion on the persuader's family.

This will be a personal chapter. It's my story. I told it first to Wheaton College faculty and students at one of our chapel services. The storm of reaction I received showed that my situation wasn't unique. These folks found it helpful to openly consider the family problems of "The Great Christian Persuader." I hope you will too. And so with a few minor variations, here are the remarks I shared with them.

* * * *

There's a popular song sung by Harry Chapin which hit the top of the charts a few years ago. It's called, "Cat's in the Cradle."[35] I'm going to run through the lyrics because they represent what I want to say. The words go like this:

My child arrived just the other day;
He came to the world in the usual way,
But there were planes to catch, and bills to pay.
He learned to walk while I was away.
And he was talkin' 'fore I knew it and as he grew,
He'd say, "I'm gonna be like you, Dad,
You know I'm gonna be like you."

Chorus
And the cat's in the cradle and the silver spoon,
Little boy blue and the man in the moon.
"When you coming home, Dad?" "I don't know when, but
We'll get together then;
You know we'll have a good time then."

My son turned ten just the other day,
He said, "Thanks for the ball, Dad, come on let's play,
Can you teach me to throw?" I said, "Not today,
I got a lot to do." He said, "That's okay."
And he, he walked away but his smile never dimmed.
It said, "I'm gonna be like him, yeah,
You know I'm gonna be like him."

Chorus

And he came from college just the other day;
So much like a man I just had to say,
"Son, I'm proud of you, can you sit for a while?"
He shook his head and he said with a smile,
"What I'd really like, Dad, is to borrow the car keys.
See you later, can I have them please?"

Chorus

I've long since retired, my son's moved away.
I called him up just the other day.
I said, "I'd like to see you if you don't mind."
He said, "I'd love to, Dad, if I can find the time.
You see my new job's a hassle and the kids have the flu,
But it's sure nice talkin' to you, Dad,
It's been sure nice talkin' to you."

And as I hung up the phone it occurred to me,
He'd grown up just like me;
My boy was just like me.

Chorus

And the cat's in the cradle and the silver spoon,
Little boy blue and the man in the moon.
"When you comin' home, Son?" "I don't know when,
But we'll get together then,
Dad, we're gonna have a good time then."

That's my story. I was raised in a home where my parents loved me, but my father was very success-oriented. In fact, I was brought up with the idea that it was my duty to get to the top in whatever I did. My father worked with a newspaper. He started as an ad salesman. Appropriately enough for Chicago in the 1930s, the first ad he sold was for a tailor shop. It said, "We mend bullet holes." He rose up through the ranks of the paper and became business manager. He was shooting for publisher, but he never quite made it. He died a broken man.

But this idea of getting to the top was infused into me. I remember one time our phone didn't work, and my dad's solution was to call the president of Illinois Bell. Go to the top! Of course as a result of this

"Congratulations, Mr. Dellington! You've made it to the top."

quest, my dad wasn't around very much. He was too busy climbing. It happened just like Chapin sings in the song. One time my folks gave me a baseball glove for my birthday. I wanted to play catch, but he was so tied up we had to schedule it for later. We planned to play a week from Saturday, and we actually started. But after about three throws he got a call and had to go down to the office.

Now the song is my story as a father too. I came to know the Lord my senior year of high school and soon decided that God was calling me into a Christian vocation. I went to seminary and joined the full-time staff of Young Life. Although it sounds conceited to say, I was one of the rising young stars of the organization. I was sent to the Wheaton area in the early 1960s to train college kids to do club work. For a new staff man, the job was a real plum. Here I was sent to take over the supervision of twelve Young Life clubs, replacing a top-notch staff man with ten years experience. I knew that the Lord wanted me to do well. He wanted me to rise up to the top—for him, of course.

Jeanie and I used to kid about the Young Life ladder I was scaling. Our laughter was a bit hollow. You started out as a club kid—someone who didn't know the Lord. After you became a Christian you were a Campaigner kid—this was a step up the ladder. If you went to college and became a volunteer leader, you were higher yet. Going to seminary and getting paid to work raised you into the category of student staff. The first year on staff you were a staff trainee, and then came full-time staff. This was followed by higher rungs on the ladder. Area Director—Metropolitan Area Director—then Regional Director—Executive Director—God! I say it facetiously, but I was working up that ladder. After three years on staff, I was Area Director and just about ready to make the jump to head of a Metropolitan Area.

All this took its toll though. I was out of the house every night of the week. Occasionally I'd take a day off and be in at night, but even when I was home physically I had checked out mentally. My mind was whirling with plans to help others. I was doing God's work—I thought. I got lots of invitations to speak. I like to speak. There's something very ego-building about having the eyes of an audience fixed upon you as you're sending forth truth. People would come to me and say, "Em, you have to talk to our group," or "The conference won't go without you. You're the only one who can do it." And I would modestly bow my head and say, "I guess that's right. OK, I'll do it."

I felt guilty about the time away from Jean and our newborn son, however, and this guilt turned me into a sneak. Many times I agreed to

"I'm on my way to dispatch two dragons, dethrone a soulless tyrant, and rescue the Grail—I'll try to catch you on the way back."

speak or lead discussion groups, but I wouldn't tell her ahead of time. I'd wait until just before and then spring it on her. This way she couldn't object—it was already scheduled and I had to go. I'd conclude my explanation to her with the words, "I've got to go. I just gotta." Not only was that bad English, it was bad for our relationship.

As I look back, I recall talking to Lars Granberg who was a psychologist and counselor at Fuller Seminary when I was there. Lars told me that he'd seen dozens of the seminary wives during the course of the year. Almost all of them had the same plaintive question. "Why am I last? My husband's studies, his church work, and his job all come before me. Why?" And Lars really couldn't answer. Now I'm quite familiar with the old bromide that it's not the quantity of time you spend with your family that makes the difference, it's the quality. As long as the quality of time is good, it's all okay. To this I say, "Nonsense!" If there's not a quantity of time, there's no quality. Of course it's possible to have great gobs of time together with your wife and kids and still have a lousy relationship—but without quantity, there's no hope of quality.

There came a night in Jeanie's and my marriage when all this came to a head. It started out typically enough. I had been away at a three-day conference and had taken a plane back early so that I could speak to a church group. Then I came home thoroughly exhausted and plopped into bed. In a despairing voice Jeanie said, "Em, I know you still love me, but I don't feel it any more, and it's hard to feel love for you anymore either"—and all of a sudden my world came crashing in.

You see, I was always a person that needed someone to love them hard. All through college I was looking for someone to marry. It usually works the other way around—the girl is looking and the guy is foot-loose. But not me. I was more serious than the gals I dated, and I was the one who got jilted. And then I found Jeanie. Here was someone who loved me hard. She was willing to be completely mine, and I completely hers. The Lord brought us together, and I knew this marriage was right. So with this background, you can see how that one sentence from Jeanie sent my world spinning.

I think I needed the props kicked out from under me to shake me loose from my "get to the top" pattern. I suddenly recalled that five years before, Jeanie and I had stood at the head of the longest aisle in the world. Before God and many witnesses I had promised that Jeanie would be the number one person in my life—that I would love, cherish, and honor her. I said that I would care for and serve her the way that Christ loved and served his church. And it dawned on me that it hadn't been so. I realized that I had to change my whole life—I had to go off Young Life staff.

Now please don't lob stones at Young Life. It wasn't the job that was at fault. It was my messed-up approach to it. I wanted to be the great Christian man, and I had built up an image in my mind that this meant frantically dashing around persuading kids. I had the warped view that it was wrong to slow down. Strange, but when I went off staff my Young Life club went better than it ever had before. I decided to keep a hand in working with the local kids. All of a sudden more kids met the Lord and the commitment of the Christians was deeper. I think it had something to do with the fact that I became more of a real person. Instead of seeing some kind of teenage Jesus, a self-appointed messiah who was out to save the world, kids saw a family man. I was more credible because I'd say, "I'm at dinner, I'll call you back," or "No, I can't do that, my wife needs me." I was a more authentic and honest person—the type maybe they wanted their own father to be.

But this is getting ahead of the story. That night I decided to go off Young Life staff. I gave six months' notice and left the work on September 30, 1966. That same day Jeanie experienced a complete emotional breakdown. She was in the hospital for two months, and for the first half of that time I didn't know whether I was going to get a wife back or not. The doctor described what happened this way: "Your absence has laid a real pressure on Jean. She's been holding herself together on nervous energy alone. When you were officially through with your job, she felt like she could relax—you'd finally be home now. And everything just came apart. It's the system's way of saying it's had enough."

God was good. Jeanie regained her health better than ever. But this was an amazing time. It was a time when I had to reorder my priorities. I had always thought that I was the strong one in our marriage, but I suddenly found how much I needed her. I also discovered what a poor mother substitute I was for the kids.

Why am I telling you all this? Because if I was stupid enough to cause this, you might make the same mistake. As Christians, we believe we have a purpose in life. We're not just drifting. I don't know of a more motivated group of people than the students of Wheaton College. Take a look at our alumni. They are influential pastors, leaders in Christian organizations all around the world, or they run their businesses as to the Lord. We're talking about a highly motivated, successful group of people. But there's a subtle danger here. It's very easy for the influential Christian to get so wrapped up in a mission to others that he does dirt to his own family. We've had some beautiful men of God come to speak to us here in chapel. I talked to one of those who is most appreciated when he comes on campus. I confessed some jealousy to him. I said, "I would like to be like you—the persuasive Christian leader who moves vast audiences. I envy you, but I couldn't do what you do because of the time I need to spend with my family. How do you handle this?" His face fell and he said simply, "I don't. I'm an absentee father, and I've got to start working on that."

I've seen this happen over and over again. Too many sons and daughters of great Christian men aren't great. They're miserable and they feel cheated that their dad was never around to minister to them. We sing, "Faith of Our Fathers," but with a little neglect it can turn into hate of our fathers, or at least a bitterness toward anything they hold. In Ephesians 5 Paul cautions, "Fathers, don't provoke your children to wrath." The best way I know to prod them in this direction is to be absent—to be out working with other people all the time and never having a time when they come first.

This isn't a problem just for Christians. The absentee father is a well-known phenomenon in the business world. The missing mother is, too. But it's a special problem for the Christian because of the temptation to rationalize the lack of family time as God's will. The non-Christian can't do this. Suppose he's out six nights a week selling used cars. His wife says, "I want you home more often." He says it's just not possible. If there's going to be money for a TV, a fur coat, and a Florida vacation, he's got to be down at the lot hustling. At this point the issue is joined. His wife can say, "We can do without the TV, I don't want a fur coat, and we can skip Florida this year. I want you home more often." And they'll have to work with the problem on this level. It's a lot tougher for the Christian wife to say, "I need you. The kids need you.'' How does she say this without sounding like she's opposing God's work or even God himself? The feelings of guilt this raises keep many women silent—and the marriage grows colder. I thank God that Jeanie loved me enough to take the risk and bring the issue to the surface.

Ethics has to do with choice. Animals don't have to worry about ethics. They don't have any choice; they go by instinct. They automatically react. But God made us to be responsible human beings—to exercise choice. My aim is to sensitize you to some decisions that you as a Christian leader must face. Perhaps the first choice involves whether or not you should get married. If God really has a special vocational ministry for you, maybe you should take Paul's admonition seriously and consider not being married. I guarantee that being married and having a family in the way that God intended takes lots of time. It's beautiful time—but it's time unavailable for the other work. If marriage is for you—as it is for me—then this means making lots of choices. It's not a matter of making one big ''once and for all'' decision; we're called on to say yes or no many times a day. I'm slowly learning that saying no can be just as Christian as saying yes. Let me close with two examples along that line.

A good friend from the University of Michigan is now a medical missionary in Bangladesh. When he arrived on the field, they told him that his four kids would have to go away to boarding school. It was mission policy—he had no choice. His response was, ''Sure I have a choice! Our kids need us. Evangelization in the home first, then on the mission field.'' He raised some money, recruited a teacher, and there's now a thriving mission school on the hospital grounds.

I got a call a few years back from a gal asking me to come speak at a dorm Bible study. She told me that they wanted me to tell them what kind of woman a Christian wife should be. I replied, ''I don't honestly know what the Christian wife is supposed to be like. Maybe you should check with Jeanie on that. But I do know what God expects of the Christian husband. And I'm afraid I'm going to have to pass up the invite this time because I've already been out three nights this week.'' There was silence for a moment and then she exclaimed, ''You mean you don't have anything else scheduled and you still won't come?'' She had trouble understanding this and finally hung up puzzled. But I felt a certain inner satisfaction that I was beginning to mature in the faith by exercising responsible choice. I had outward satisfaction too. Right after I got off the phone my son climbed into my arms and gave me a kiss. He said simply, ''Thanks, Dad.''

Martin Luther King had a slogan he once used for a rally. It said, ''If you care, you'll be there.'' That's not bad. I think it applies to the family. If you really care about them, you'll be around. The truly great Christian man will be great first in his own home.

Postscript

I'm writing this on the day before Christmas. It's been three years almost to the day since I started this book. It's hard to remain static during that long a period of time. Occasionally I've found that I have to go back and revise something I wrote early in the game. It no longer seems true, I have new information, or its importance has changed. But my overall attitude toward the process of Christian persuasion remains unaltered. In fact, the events of these three years have only strengthened my commitment to that approach. On the chance that I've done a lousy job and fogged it by, let me summarize my view:

People are human beings, not souls to be won. They are valuable for who they are, not merely for the responses they may make. People bruise easily. We must be careful not to fold, spindle, or mutilate. If we don't come on like gangbusters, but are willing to take some time and be sensitive to where another person is at, we can usually win a hearing for our beliefs. If we take care to present the advantages of our position in an open, unambiguous, and winsome way, there's a good chance others will freely respond. We need to stick with a person after he accepts our advice so that he doesn't revert back to lack of support. And finally, we must be willing to change and grow ourselves.

These things I believe. I hope I've persuaded you.

Notes

1. C. S. Lewis, *The Abolition of Man* (Copyright 1944, 1947 by Macmillan Publishing Co., Inc., renewed 1972, 1975 by Alfred Cecil Harwood and Arthur Owen Barfield) page 309. Used by permission of the publisher.
2. Harvey Cox, *The Seduction of the Spirit* (New York: Simon and Schuster, 1973), page 309. Used by permission of the publisher.
3. Gordon W. Allport and Leo J. Postman, "The Basic Psychology of Rumor," from *Readings in Social Psychology*, Third Edition by Eleanor E. Maccoby, Theodore M. Newcomb, and Eugene L. Hartley (New York: Holt, Rinehart and Winston, 1958) pages 54-64.
4. Jack W. Brehm, *A Theory of Psychological Reactance* (New York: Academic Press, 1966).
5. Leon Festinger and N. Maccoby, "On Resistance to Persuasive Communications," *Journal of Abnormal Social Psychology*, 1964, Vol. 68, pages 359-366.
6. Emory A. Griffin, "The Effects of Varying Degrees of Audience Density Upon Auditor Attitude," An unpublished dissertation submitted to Northwestern University, Evanston, Illinois, June, 1971.
7. J. M. Carlsmith and A. E. Gross, "Some Effects of Guilt on Compliance," *Journal of Personality and Social Psychology*, 11, 1969, 232-39.
8. Paul Tournier, *Guilt and Grace* (New York: Harper and Row, 1962), pages 17, 18. Used by permission of the publisher.
9. K. L. Higbee, "Fifteen Years of Fear Arousal: Research on Threat Appeals," *Psychological Bulletin*, 1969, Vol. 72, pages 426-444.
10. I. L. Janis, and L. Mann, "Effectiveness of Emotional Roleplaying in Modifying Smoking Habits and Attitudes," *Journal of Experimental Research in Personality*, 1965, Vol. 1, pages 84-90.
11. This is an actual case of shaping. See B. F. Skinner, *About Behaviorism* (New York: Alfred A. Knopf, 1974) for a further discussion.

12. Keith Miller, *The Becomers* (Waco, Texas: Word Books, 1973), pages 89-99.
13. I. P. Pavlov, *Lectures on Conditioned Reflexes*, Vol. 2. *Conditioned Reflexes and Psychiatry*. Trans. Horsley Gantt (London: Lawrence & Wishart, 1941).
14. I. L. Janis, D. Kaye, and P. Kirschner, "Facilitating Effects of 'Eating-While-Reading' on Responsiveness to Persuasive Communications," *Journal of Personality and Social Psychology*, 1, 1965, 181-86.
15. K. E. Anderson, and T. A. Clevenger, "A Summary of Experimental Research in Ethos," *Speech Monographs*, 1963, Vol. 30, pages 59-78.
16. Carl I. Hovland, Irving L. Janis, and Harold H. Kelley, *Communication and Persuasion*, (New Haven: Yale University Press, 1953), pages 19-55.
17. Paul Krieger, and Dan Veltman, "My Dog, Your Dog," (unpublished paper).
18. Leon Festinger, *A Theory of Cognitive Dissonance* (Stanford University Press, 1957), pages 123-176.
19. Shirley A. Star and Helen M. Hughes, "Report on an Educational Campaign: The Cincinnati Plan for the United Nations," *American Journal of Sociology*, 1950, Vol. 55, pages 389-400.
20. Marshall McLuhan, *The Medium is the Message* (New York: Random House, Inc., 1967).
21. R. K. Merton, *Mass Persuasion* (New York: Harper, 1946), p. 189.
22. *The Miami Herald*, February 16, 1975, page 20-G.
23. E. Katz, "The Two-Step Flow of Communication: An Up-To-Date Report on an Hypothesis," *Public Opinion Quarterly*, 1957, Vol. 21, pages 61-78.
24. Excerpt from *The Responsive Chord* by Tony Schwartz. Copyright © 1973 by Anthony Schwartz. Reprinted by permission of Doubleday & Company, Inc., page 93.
25. William J. McGuire, "Inducing Resistance to Persuasion," from *Advances in Experimental Social Psychology*, Volume 1, edited by Leonard Berkowitz (New York): Academic Press, 1964), pages 192-231.
26. Richard LaPiere, "Attitudes Vs. Actions," *Social Forces*, 13, 1934, 230-237.
27. Donald T. Campbell, "Social Attitudes and Other Acquired Behavioral Dispositions," *In Psychology: A Study of Science*, Volume 6, edited by S. Koch (New York: McGraw-Hill, 1963), 94-172.
28. Richard L. Miller, Philip Brickman, and Diana Bolen, "Attribution Versus Persuasion as a Means for Modifying Behavior," *Journal of Personality and Social Psychology*, Vol. 31, Number 3, March 1975, pages 430-441.
29. J. L. Freedman, and S. C. Fraser, "Compliance Without Pressure: The Foot-in-the Door Technique," *Journal of Personality and Social Psychology*, 4, 1966, 195-202.
30. Daryl J. Bem, *Beliefs, Attitudes, and Human Affairs* (Belmont, California: Brooks/Cole Publishing Co., 1970), pages 57-69.
31. S. Asch, "Effects of Group Pressure Upon the Modification and Distortion of Judgment," *Groups, Leadership, and Men*, edited by H. Guetzkow (Pittsburgh: The Carnegie Press, 1951).
32. D. Campbell, "Conformity in Psychology's Theories of Acquired Behavioral Disposition," in *Conformity and Deviation*, edited by I. Berg and R. Bass (New York, 1961), pages 101-142.
33. T. M. Newcomb, "Persistence and Regression of Changed Attitudes: Long Range Studies," *Journal of Social Issues*, Vol. 19, 1963, pages 3-14.
34. M. Sherif, *The Psychology of Social Norms* (New York: Harper and Row, 1963).
35. "Cat's in the Cradle" © 1974 Story Songs Ltd. All rights reserved. Words by Harry Chapin and Sandy Chapin. Used by permission.